CW00517303

POETRY COMPE1

GREAT MINDS

Your World...Your Future...YOUR WORDS

From Gloucestershire

Edited by Kelly Oliver

 Young**Writers**

First published in Great Britain in 2005 by:
Young Writers
Remus House
Coltsfoot Drive
Peterborough
PE2 9JX
Telephone: 01733 890066
Website: www.youngwriters.co.uk

SB ISBN 1 84460 698 8

Foreword

This year, the Young Writers' 'Great Minds' competition proudly presents a showcase of the best poetic talent selected from over 40,000 up-and-coming writers nationwide.

Young Writers was established in 1991 to promote the reading and writing of poetry within schools and to the youth of today. Our books nurture and inspire confidence in the ability of young writers and provide a snapshot of poems written in schools and at home by budding poets of the future.

The thought, effort, imagination and hard work put into each poem impressed us all and the task of selecting poems was a difficult but nevertheless enjoyable experience.

We hope you are as pleased as we are with the final selection and that you and your family continue to be entertained with *Great Minds From Gloucestershire* for many years to come.

Contents

Barnwood Park High School

Churchdown School

Stephanie Whalley (12)	53
Howard Colin (13)	54
Richard Aunger (12)	54
Sean Baker (13)	55
Maria-Eléna Ridgway (13)	56
Sam Cooper (14)	57
Bronwen Scales (12)	58
Martyn Edward Adamson (11)	58
Charlotte Lewis (12)	59
Sophie Davis (11)	59
Chantelle Ali (11)	60
Tom Allen (11)	60
Jodie Louise Witts (11)	61
Emily Hyett (12)	61
Ryan Lowe (12)	62
Samantha Reed (12)	62
Emily Trigg (12)	63
Sam Myatt (12)	63
Ross Goodhall (12)	64
Gareth Jones (12)	64
Andy Knight (13)	65
Sophie Grimes (12)	65
Ashley Mott (12)	66
Ramon Thomas (12)	66
Ami Ward (11)	67
Stuart Stephenson (13)	67
Tiffany Lowery (14)	68
Chevez Smith (12)	68
Suzanna Richards (12)	69
Holly Reynolds (11)	69
Nick Pugh (12)	70
Lee Russell (11)	70
Sean Mobley (11)	70
Billy Poulter (12)	71
Joe Lawrence (13)	71
Katie Evans (11)	72
Nicole Lewis (12)	72
Louise Lewin (12)	73
Edward Durrant (13)	73
Daniel Marks (11)	73

Kimberley Iliffe (12)	74
Sam Large (12)	74
Jake O'Malley (11)	75
Jordan Kline (12)	75
Debbie Hayes (12)	76
Haydon King (11)	76
Kyle Coe (12)	76
Matthew Etchells (12)	77
Daniel Weir (11)	77
Liam Shotbolt (11)	78
Bradley Hall (11)	78
Ross Wheeler (12)	78
Suzanne Murray (14)	79
Shane Trigg (12)	79
Samuel Wheeler (11)	80
Jade Stacey (11)	80
Siobhan How (13)	81
George Richards (11)	81
Samantha Cooper (11)	82
Jenny Humphris (11)	82
Harry Lewis (13)	82
Zoe Hitchen (13)	83
Bethan Morgan (13)	83
Adam Leach (13)	84
Louis Fawl (11)	84
Shane Deeley (11)	84
Louisa Gorman (13)	85
Sam Hancock (13)	85
George Evans (11)	86
Becky Nash (13)	86
Jack Christmas (11)	87
Ryan Deas (11)	87
Dominic Vanstone (13)	87
Kelly Whitmore (13)	88
Tom Willetts (11)	88
Bridie Banon (11)	89
Timothy Campbell (11)	89
Adam Brain (12)	90
Craig Bolton (11)	90
Bethan Petersen (12)	90
Charlotte Smith (11)	91
Faye Warner (11)	91

Tanya Mutingwende (11)   92
Alice Prince (11)   92

Newent Community School
Lauren Wilden (13)   93
Micky Whittle (13)   93
Harriet Baynham-Williams (13)   94
Luke Warren (14)   94
Lucy Henderson (12)   95
Jo Daly (12)   96
Rebecca Overbury (12)   97
Jess Huggins (12)   98
Susanna Nolan (13)   99
Rupert Bailey (12)   100
Harrianne Burdett (12)   101
Rachel Hobby (13)   102
Will Voss (13)   103
Chris Dowle (12)   104
Harriet Evans (13)   105
Jennifer Walker (13)   106
Emily Padley (12)   107
Gemma Prince (12)   108
Thomas Farr (15)   109
Matthew Ward (12)   110
Cheryl Cooper (13)   110
Hannorah Stephens (14)   111
Sarah Phillips (12)   111
Charmaine Evans (12)   112
Nicola Thurston (12)   112
Alice Murphy (13)   113
Kate Richards (13)   113
Tanya Oliver-Burns (12)   114
Chloe Hopper (12)   114
Stacey Evans (16)   115
Matt Siddle (13)   115
Amelia Cornish (12)   116
Samantha Brockbank (12)   116
Francesca Moss (12)   117
Jess Butler (13)   117

Ribston Hall High School

The Cotswold School

Melissa Ridgway (13)	185
Lucy Clark (11)	186
Maizey Roberts (13)	186
Clair Akhurst (15)	187
Carly Woodward (13)	187
James Hopkins (13)	188
Lisa Brown (11)	188
Megan Warren (15)	189
Yssy Baker (15)	189
Jenny Adams (12)	190
Emily Nobes (11)	190
Georgia Wood (11)	191
Hayden Scamp (11)	191
Shona Corbett (11)	192
Joe Jenkins (13)	192
Hannah Chappell (11)	193
Lara Crook (13)	193
Katie-Lousie Churchill (11)	194
Harley-Ray Hill (11)	194
Jess Hendy (15)	195
Isaac McMorrow (12)	196
Megan Laws (11)	196
Richard Townsend (12)	197
Ashley Kent (11)	197
Hannah Bucknell (11)	198
Darren Brocklehurst (11)	198
Shannon Absalom (13)	199
Jordan Day (11)	199
Sam Underwood (13)	200
John-Paul Crawford (11)	200
Jimmy Bower (13)	201
Sophie Kerry (13)	201
Jack Marshall (13)	202
Angharad England (13)	202
Gabriel Raeburn (13)	203
Christine Irving (12)	203
Lucy Wise (11)	204
Henry Walker (12)	204
Amy Holder (14)	205
Jay Newman (12)	205
Sean Box (12)	206
Jake Rogers (13)	206

The Poems

An Ode To www.jellybabies.com

O' to the site that showed me
Just how fantastic they can be
These great Jelly Babies
Without any ifs, buts or maybes
How pleased I was to see
However mouldy they may be
A collection of jelly heads
All looking very much dead.

O' to the ways of eating
Jelly Babies in a meeting
Devour, bite or nibble
The head, leg or the middle
Decapitation of babies
Is by child-bearing ladies
And eating a baby in one
By childless women is done.

O' to the screaming torture
Potassium chlorate vulture
The baby-burning reflection
Of candyfloss complexion
Melting, dissolving and dying
Jelly Baby soon be flying
They are more than just a snack
Excitement they never lack.

O' to the figures and facts
Jelly knowledge will not lack
Jelly Baby fans will all know
The magic that lives below
All the crispy outer shells
Of the babies made from gel
So watch out for a bite
So tremendous is this site.

Helen Jackson (15)
Balcarras School

Journey

All the people, all the places,
All the sadness on all the faces.
So little time, to see the world,
But on I must go, my sail unfurled.

My own little tour, of the life I lead,
Shooting along at breakneck speed.
But we all know some day that my tour must stop,
And into the gutter you'll see me flop.

No longer a child, but an established opinion,
Living my life, I'm my own little minion.
Life is a journey, with its highs and its lows,
Just like a river, it ebbs and it flows.

All of my life is entirely your doing -
The good and the bad, the starts and the stops.
But it was fun.
Thanks for my journey.

Ben Lane (13)
Balcarras School

My Sweet Tree

If I had a sweet tree,
Bonbons it would hold.
Lots of sweets for you and me
From places new and old!

Red, blue, green and gold,
Are the colours it would hoard,
So many different types of sweets,
You never could get bored!

Humbugs and toffees,
Lemon and lime chews,
Chocolates and mints,
Make it so hard to choose!

Hannah Bourne (13)
Balcarras School

Winter

Squirrels hoard their nuts in May,
Ready for that winter's day,
When cold sweeps through cobbled streets,
When the beggar sits and weeps and weeps.
The trees shed their leaves and shiver in the cold,
Waiting to mature and become dead and old.
The landlord shouts, 'Come and eat my stew.'
But they all fear the grass, wet with dew.
The rich kid sleeps in a bed of silk,
The poor kid sleeps with nothing but milk.
In her heart the chill creeps in,
Waiting for her next of kin.
She falls to the ground,
The snow breaks her fall.
Dead in the darkness,
She feels chill no more.

Hope Sanders (13)
Balcarras School

You

I want you, I need you, I love you, I breathe you,
Every time that I leave you,
I grieve for you.

If I could have you near me,
Just for you to hear me,
I long for you to steer me
Back down the path of love.

I hate you, I loathe you, but I love you and I need you,
You're *my* obsession,
Long to be in your possession.

I don't care what they say,
Just one minute feels like a day,
When we are apart - it shatters my heart.

Want me, need me, love me, breathe me too.

Livvie Davis (13)
Balcarras School

Falcon

I sit, motionless, in the wood, eyes tightly closed
No action, no falsifying dream
The whisper of the wind, envelops a hooked head
A tear, squeezed out by the breeze, becomes a crystal.

The convenient shelter of the autumn cape
The sunburst and buoyant air, is my advantage
And the view of the Earth, my dinner plate
A wink of my eye, a target is caught in sight.

My feet clasp the flaking bark
Each branch, an individual creation
Each delicate feather, an individual creation
A tool of mine to slice through air, descending upon prey.

A climactic end, a swift laceration to the flesh
Not a murmur, not a squeal, no crisp leaf falls
A slaughter, slaying of an innocent equal
Death comes to us all, all we can do is wait.

James Purveur (15)
Balcarras School

A Day At The Seaside

I was walking along the bay,
wondering what I might see.
Thinking *what will I do today?*
The seaside looks very good to me.

I tried building bundles of sand,
using a bucket and spade.
D12 were playing as a band,
paying money for a trade.

The tide was on its way inwards,
because of the daily thing.
Time for me to go, I'm bored,
I will go use a seagull's wing.

Craig Baker (13)
Balcarras School

The World Today

The world today,
Is run by religion and belief,
Mad people forcing their ways,
Upon others in grief.

They have guns,
They have bombs,
They don't think they're doing wrong,
Although the psychos from 9/11
Knew all along,

That the day of the attack,
Heaven's gate would be packed,
And how could they think,
Destruction's a godly act?

Martyr for a cause,
Or so they say,
The 9/11 men,
Are the plague of today.

Tom Hackwell (15)
Balcarras School

Mystery

Why do you come here each year?
All you do is bring cold and fear
What do you get from being hated
And killing those who have been created?
Runaway people scream, for they fear what you dream,
Make us shiver, make us shake,
Release from your cold, hard wake
Here we are, trapped in your hell
Please release us from this shell.

Harry Marrick (14)
Balcarras School

Hallowe'en

Hallowe'en is coming
So you'd better watch your step
The bogeyman is humming
Humming the song of death

He hides behind the door
He sleeps under your bed
He creeps along the floor
And scares you till you're dead

And if you fail to die right there
Run away if you dare
He will get there faster than you
You will scream and not know what to do

He comes every Hallowe'en
He loves to hear little girls scream
As he shuffles on to his house
He might see *you* next year so watch out!

Catherine Hardisty (14)
Balcarras School

A Strange Sort Of Rain

Out of her eyelids it poured,
And through her heart she stabbed a sword.
Clutching the letter he wrote,
Importance of that little note.
A teardrop fell softly down,
and in her tears she'll finally drown.

And now she's dead he's to blame,
Without her love he is left lame.
Holding her hand in his own,
He swallowed the pills with a moan.
Her voice, whispered, now calling,
And all around rain is falling.

Alicia Sutton-Jennings (13)
Balcarras School

English Lesson

It was quarter to twelve in 1A3,
Mrs Flood was screaming,
'You do your poem and then you'll be free,'
And then she hit the ceiling.

Steph was working very hard and,
Clement was looking like death,
Mrs Flood held up her high hand,
'Ssshhh,' she muttered under her breath.

Carrie was writing about Christmas,
Cat about Hallowe'en,
Devon was told not to make a fuss,
Or Mr Healy would be seen.

That was English on Monday,
All work, no play!

Lauren Gallagher (13)
Balcarras School

Inescapable

A light bulb flickering off and on,
A squeaky floorboard in the cellar,
A creepy corridor miles long,
A thought of scary life and terror.

A high-pitched voice in the next room up,
A sudden sound of a banging gun,
A killing of a newborn pup.
Thoughts of happiness I have none.

But this sad life is normal for me,
I'm always trapped alone in here,
Terror and torture is all I see,
'Cause in your own head there's only fear!

Joanne Richell (14)
Balcarras School

The Three Little Pigs - A Happy Tail

(Inspired by the story of 'The Three Little Pigs')

'You're big pigs now,' their mother had said,
Before she kicked them out of bed.
'You're on your own, the time has come,
To live by yourselves and have lots of fun.'

They crept outside into the night,
Their tiny pink bodies filled with fright.
They walked along, what should they do?
The experience was all brand new.

They saw the sun rise at dawn,
As the smallest pig stifled a yawn.
The eldest said, like a brave knight,
'Don't worry little pigs, we will be alright.'

The fearless pigs bumped into a man,
Who tried to sell straw to the clan.
The smallest pig, filled with glee,
Bought some straw quite happily.

He hugged his brothers and said goodbye,
Trying very hard not to cry.
The others were sad, but carried on,
And soon saw the man walking along.

He offered the pigs a bundle of sticks,
But the oldest pig wanted some bricks.
The second pig took the lot,
But the wisest little pig did not.

So the eldest piggy said goodbye,
Wiping a tear from his eye.
The oldest pig was on his own,
The rest had gone to build a home.

His head bowed down, he walked alone,
When from the side he heard a moan.
He turned to look, and on his right,
Was a pile of bricks, to his delight.

A man straightened up from under the pile,
He gave them to the pig with a smile.
With all the bricks loaded on his back,
The pig set off along the track.

Now the first pig had built his home,
Compete with a red garden gnome.
The second pig's house of sticks,
Was finished along with the house of bricks.

The pigs lived there for years to come,
Always having lots of fun.
The piggies' homes were filled with laughter,
And they lived happily ever after.

Eleanor Baker (14)
Balcarras School

Death

Death the end of it all
Where do we go?
Life seems so small
We have to let go.

Lives are lost
Heaven or Hell
My body far from the frost
My body has fell.

I lie under six feet of earth
Pale and cold
A world without mirth
My body never got frail and old.

Buried alive in the dark
Left here with only my regrets
In my life I've left a mark
I breathe my last breath and die.

Sam Crow (13)
Balcarras School

Busy Schedule

We rush home
on busy schedules
in our busy lives
grab a bite to eat
kiss the wife on the head
and stroke the baby's hand
then leave to earn more money
we run around the shops
grabbing dilapidated bottles of milk
and throwing cash at the checker
then running to the muddy car
wiping muddy feet on already-caked mats
driving 90 miles an hour down the motorway
stopping to look for a present
for the dreaded in-laws
who were haphazardly invited
the day drags by in a whirlpool
of rubbing Vaseline on swollen knuckles
head slumped over the flat screen computer
trying to catch enough sleep
to keep going
and not to scream or shout
at people who don't deserve it
getting home, the wife nagging
you bought the wrong milk
the fridge is broken, frozen food everywhere
the baby crying and the Hoover left untended
the television toppling over, and the wife
sitting at home all day reading, 'Woman's Own'
and cuddling the first-born child, the mini person
and you find yourself screaming
screaming and shouting and raging

in the end you slap her round the face
the baby still crying, the Hoover still left,
and feeling like a s***, feeling the guilt
and slumping down and crying
making time to feel emotions
after rushing home
in this busy schedule
in this busy life.

Isobel Blaikie (15)
Balcarras School

Footsteps In The Snow

You plant flowers in the garden,
You leave footsteps in the snow,
But when you no longer walk the Earth,
What is left to show?

Flowers die in winter,
And snow will thaw in spring,
But if your ears no longer hear,
How can they hear birds sing?

Children after children,
Daughter after son,
Who is there to mourn you
When your final breath has gone?

If nothing lasts forever,
And everyone must die,
Will you only leave a gravestone,
Between the ground and sky?

Francesca Gibbons (15)
Balcarras School

In The Pits

It lay gleaming in the light
The artificial spotlights humming
The advertisements trying with all their might
To get the people running
To buy their products quickly
Then engine's pistons zooming
Up and down the cylinders thickly
The crankshaft's limit looming
As the revs rise to their max
The red line gets closer
The side exit exhausts thunder
The tyres strain to control the power
The engineers make the final suspension tweak
Vroom! Vroom!
The noise makes even the bravest go weak . . .

Matt Hodges (14)
Balcarras School

Trouble

The sun was shining,
The water was glistening,
My mum was ironing,
And I was kissing.

My day was all but sad,
Me and my friends,
We weren't that bad,
We bought a Mercedes Benz.

The plastic was bright,
We were not,
We all saw the light,
On our yacht.

Lloyd Whittaker (14)
Balcarras School

Dopeyo

One day Dopeyo was walking down a lane,
His ankle overcame with pain.
It throbbed and it throbbed until he was blue,
He asked his lawyer if he should sue!
He went to the hospital to ask for a crutch,
Then he thought it was too much.
He tied it to a rocket that went to space,
Then he fell over his flippin' lace.

He had a really, really bad cut,
It even shocked his ancient mutt.
So he bandaged his wound up with a newspaper,
And then he had a pizza with a caper.
After that he was refreshed,
But then he got tangled in a mesh.
After that he just gave up,
So then he had a 7Up.

David Kelly (11)
Balcarras School

The Knotted Tree

At the bottom of the garden
Stood the knotted tree

Bending and creaking
Just for me

Like a grandad
Creaking in time

Howling and shrieking
To the beat of a chime

His startling eyes so bright and smooth
Dancing and singing to the beat of the groove

Slowly swaying to the silent sun
The buds are bursting, spring has begun.

Imogen Naylor-Higgs (11)
Balcarras School

Left Alone

A slum of a cottage,
Lies on a cliff,
Looking out to sea.
There lives an old woman.
Her skin shows her age.
As she gazes out of the broken window,
Her memories rush through her.
Her happy, lively childhood.
Full of smiles and laughter.
Playing in the sun all day long.
Not a care,
Not an ounce of worry.
But now there is no one.
No one to care for,
No one to care for her.
Where did they all go?
Why have they all gone
And left her,
All alone?

Alyssa Bethell (15)
Balcarras School

The Cobra

As it streaks through the grass floor
Like a torpedo running along the seabed,
Without a single word of warning . . .
It pounces, its fangs glaring and ready.
As it strikes, its dagger-like teeth sink into its victim
And silence, an unusual silence.
And . . . nothing!

Clem Hencher-Stevens (13)
Balcarras School

My Years

Once I had a yellow dove
And I held it with a yellow glove
When it died it went to Heaven
That all happened when I saw seven

When I was eight
I faced my fate
Of looking at slugs
Or eating bugs

When I was nine
I was feeling fine
Until one night
I had a fright
Of experiencing food poisoning

The day after that
I died wearing a hat
Now I'm in Heaven
Writing this poem.

Josh James (13)
Balcarras School

About Her Person
(Based on 'The Lady of Shalott' by Alfred Lord Tennyson)

The boat so silent as the night
The leaves upon her falling, light
It is the Lady of Shalott
The mirror, cracked, the curse revealed
The dress is pale white against the night.
The woven tapestry,
Bright finished, in her hands
Reflecting the scene he saw
Sir Lancelot gazed down, the lady still,
No words were spoken,
But tipping the bow, her name,
'The Lady of Shalott'. That was all.

Darren Crossley (13)
Balcarras School

Miss Booklover

Miss Booklover has a need
  Of reading books, she loves to read.
    She reads anything from top to toe.
      She even reads her number on her bungalow.

        Miss Booklover is kind and loving
          To children all the time.
            But can be mean and stubborn
              To kids who cross the line.

            Miss Booklover works in a library
          With lots and lots of books.
        And when she sees a book she likes
      She has a little look.

She has a special personality
  To make children adore her.
    The same personality to make
      Children never ignore her.

Laura Masling (11)
Balcarras School

About Her Person

(Based on 'The Lady of Shalott' by Alfred Lord Tennyson)

A boat, carved to look like a bird,
Intricate but somehow out of this world.
Her body, distorted, ghostly and pale,
The silence of death rung around like a bell.
Found: various pieces of glass,
Contrary to the point killing weapons were sparse,
Except for a knife - bloodless and cold,
But used for carving her name on the wall.
One thing strikes as slightly unclear,
Needles and threads as thin as hair,
Nothing else was there.

Lawrence Donohoe (14)
Balcarras School

Mr Snotchboggle

When Mr Snotchboggle was born,
The doctor was quite forlorn,
He passed out with fright,
This child was not right,
On Earth a monstrosity was born.

At an age of 53,
He does nothing but gently sip tea,
With no goals in life,
All he achieves is strife,
And not much to show for himself.

The pupils at Flangleweed school,
Are unimpressed by his attempts to look cool,
With a sticky-out chin,
And a cheesy grin,
He's hardly a sight for sore eyes.

For dinner he delves up his nose,
For afters he chews at his toes,
At home he lives on his own,
Apart from his parents, he is all alone.

Greta Megroff (11)
Balcarras School

About Her Person

(Based on 'The Lady of Shalott' by Alfred Lord Tennyson)

A knife held frozen claiming her name, her robe
White as the mist before her eyes, her hair
Red as the blood that never came, her face
Deep in the eternal sleep, his face
Full of sorrow, the tapestry complete with
Life and joy, her heart
Dark with shadows and grieving.

Love was everything to her.

James Cooke (13)
Balcarras School

In The Shadows

In the shadows of the years
Time bombs ticking unknown to our peers
The terror grows, though silenced from our ears
And Blair argues about hunting, to distract our fears

In the shadows, it's quickly said
As Donald Duck plots to kill the kids
He sends soldiers in the dark to find their beds
Welcome to the news, another shot dead

In the shadows left to sit and rot
As President Bush buys his way to the top
With his father's *oil* he bought them off
'End the war,' we cried, but we're tricked to stop

In the shadows is what some say
As we act drunken in the face of the fray
So the government continues to lead us astray
But we might learn the truth, maybe, one day.

Joe Watkins (16)
Balcarras School

I Hate You

I thought you were special, my 'one' at last
The person who could help me heal the past
I loved you like I had never before
That haze of love I had not seen before
You 'loved' me, you promised me everything
But now I am alone; I have nothing
I saw you with her, and I felt 'it' break
'It' which every day gave me an ache
Now I feel nothing, I am but a shell
Where all but one feeling remains to dwell
I lie, I can still feel the pain of two;
I love you still, but I simply hate you.

Rhiannon McNeill (15)
Balcarras School

About Her Person
(Based on 'The Lady of Shalott' by Alfred Lord Tennyson)

Down by the water,
Glass shard in her hand,
Lay the lost lover
Now free to wander
The world

Now so far above,
Looks down smiling
To the Lady of Shalott
And meets the still stare
Of bold Sir Lancelot

Her hair, in the water
Dress ripped and torn
But the smile on her face
Gives no reason to mourn
The Lady of Shalott.

Isobel Powell (13)
Balcarras School

Land Battle

Shimmering in the sunlight, gleaming like polished blue glass,
The wave moves lazily, lapping at the shore,
No more,
It grows and grows building with every second,
Gathering pace, gathering strength, gathering might,
The deep blue wave comes crashing in on the rock below,
The once mighty blue mountain is reduced to a mere wash
Among the sand,
The rock stands strong,
It retreats back once again lapping lazily at the shore,
Tamed is the great giant,
Murmurs in the wind; 'I will grow again,'
Back to crash once more,
Among your brittle, little shore.

Edward Parker (15)
Balcarras School

Poem Mush, Init.

I's got a mucka called Acer,
'E finks 'e's a bit of a boy racer,
But 'e was out rexin' last night, downtown,
When 'is car spun clean off the ground.
'E 'eard the gaffas tearin' on it,
To inspect 'is totally whacked-out spin.
Last time 'e got caught out a-crusin',
The pigs gave him a well harsh bruisin',
So'e crawled out the car, jumped over a gate,
This would be how 'e tried to escape.
Unfortunately 'e was not to be knowin',
That the owner was outside, late-night mowin'.
This chavvy, 'e smacked 'im straight on the nose,
An' tied 'im up in a dirty great hose.
When the coppers arrived, to see what was down,
They found 'im curled up, alone, on the ground.
He got locked away for just 60 days,
Then 'e was back to 'is street racin' ways.

Tony Locke (15)
Balcarras School

Miss Luvvy Doo Doo

Ballroom dancing and hearts are,
The kind of thing you would find,
When Miss Luvvy Doo Doo is around,
You will often hear her cry,
'Love me do dooooooooo.'
And that is only on good days,
Quite often you would find,
Random people dressed in hearts,
Giving out leaflets like mad,
And there would be Miss Luvvy Doo Doo shouting out,
'A date a day, you won't have to pay!'

Polly Liggett (11)
Balcarras School

The Mystic

Alone in the dark,
Ghostly white
Eyes pure grey
Without any light

She stares out at the world,
Listening to the night
Her eyes hypnotic
A mystical sight

She scares me,
Scares everyone
But no one can stop her
Not even a gun

A bullet goes through her
Fire burns out
We think she's immortal
Without a doubt

Her furniture rocks
Her bed bales of hay
She listens at night
And hunts through the day

Her life is a mystery
She came without trace
A total stranger
Betraying human race

She has no name
A cave as a home
She has no laws
She's free to roam

Her life itself is tragic
We call her Mysti Magic.

Philippa Jordan (11)
Balcarras School

Murder In The Dark

On a dark night in May,
The wind blew and howled
'Beware of the black pay,'
In the shadows stood a crowd.

In the crowd there were many thieves
All big and fat, short and stubby.
These thieves had tricks up their sleeves.
One was exceptionally chubby.

They were planning something, I think.
Was it a burglary? Was it a murder?
They got into their positions, wink, wink!
They're off into the house, 'Look out, girder.'

So it went on, I knew nothing,
Then I saw it, lying on the street bed.
There was a grey pay packet, puffing,
It saw me, 'Want some?' I was stone dead.

On a dark night in May,
The wind blew and howled
'Beware of the black pay,'
In the shadows stood a crowd.

In the crowd there were many thieves
All big and fat, short and stubby.
These thieves had tricks up their sleeves.
One was exceptionally chubby.

I watched and waited.
They could not see me.
I was no more, just a spirit,
Howling, howling
'Beware of the black pay!'

Mike Hindle (13)
Balcarras School

Ant-ics

There was an ant that lived in a nutshell on the floor,
With a carpet of moss and a spare room for
The relation, the friend and, of course, the visitor,
Who used to come knocking on his tiny door.
There was a regular called Pleasant,
Who liked to pass the time of day,
An occasional called Distant,
You see, he lived too far away,
The loudmouth called Extravagant,
Ever careless and always proud,
Or, if you're after perfection, Brilliant,
The brightest in this crowd.
The constant and helpful Tolerant,
Who gave every job a shot,
Or the prized and sought after Pheasant,
The most hunted of the lot,
An unwelcome and scheming Tyrant,
Who made sure he always got the best,
Or the hardworking and simple Peasant,
Who had to put up with the rest.
The hero of the hour was always Triumphant,
Who kept the evils and enemies at bay,
The shadow in the background was often Hesitant,
Not anxious or anticipating to stay.
The hesitant twin was Reluctant,
A shy one too,
Whilst the steadiest there was Valiant,
Always strong and true.
But these different ants all had the same reason to call,
The first ant was the most important of all.

Emma Cann (13)
Balcarras School

Time, Time, Time

I watch the clock as time goes by
I listen for the birds in the sky
I'm waiting for them to sing
And as they do so bring
Dawn

I watch the clock as time goes by
I hope that it will fly
And in doing so bring
Midday

I watch the clock as time goes by
And I try, try, not to cry
Evening has come to stay
Until for night it makes way
Evening

I watch the clock as time goes by
Night has come, it's very sly
As it takes me into its embrace
The eyes close upon my face
Night

Time, time, time, it's always there
When you're happy and when you're scared
Time.

Thomas Plastow (11)
Balcarras School

Poker Joker

Hi everybody,
I'm sure you're eager to see me,
My name is Poker Joker,
And I love playing poker.

I eat lots of grease,
Which is why I'm quite obese,
You'll see me in a woolly fleece,
So hold your nose and your cheeks.

Please get on your knees,
To prevent yourself from fleas,
Or even a lot of bees,
So I beg you, please, please.

I work as a servant,
For an old man named Mr McMervant,
I love him so,
But his feet, oh no!

So it's time for me to say goodbye,
Doesn't time fly?
Poking and joking that's all for me,
So see you around, tee hee hee!

Jemma Jones (11)
Balcarras School

www.lego.com

We always used to argue on who would get the shark,
The little road, the cannonballs and the building blocks
No matter what I did
I never got my way
As I was just the 'little girl' who shouldn't play the game

My brother got the red
My brother got the blue
He got the whites and the blacks
He even got the biggest base
And the sails too!

I had to stick with Polly Pocket, fun all around!
With little people you could barely hold
And which would snap in a matter of time

I wanted the building blocks,
I wanted all the fun
I wanted to play Lego all day
Not the pink girlie strums

Lego was a joy
Lego was all it
With Lego World and plastic people
Who wouldn't enjoy it?

Though when I did get what I wanted, guess what was included?
Pink, girly people, who looked just like Polly Pocket
But hey, who's to complain?
It was Lego after all . . .

Jenny Haynes
Balcarras School

All Muddled Up

'Confuse!' screamed the boss
'Confuse, you're ten minutes late!
What's wrong with you man?
It's twenty past eight!'

'It's one of those days, Sir!'
Confuse quickly replied,
'My head's all a muddle!
It's gone for a ride!'

'This is really not on!'
The boss fiercely cried,
'You can't keep on doing this,
You . . . are . . . fried!'

Confuse sadly walked home
To his small, mouldy flat
Sat in his chair
And stroked his cat.

'What shall I do?
My life's such a mess!
Please tell me!
Please tell me Tess.'

Confuse has a very rushed life
As you have probably worked out
Being here and there all the time
Has its enormous doubts.

Emma Campbell (12)
Balcarras School

The Mystery

(Based on 'The Lady of Shalott' by Alfred Lord Tennyson)

Drifting gracefully,
Draped the boat
A striking tapestry
A blade in her fist that carved the
Mystery.

Colour drained from her face
As she lay in grace
Everywhere
Peace

Gliding down
Entangled
In an ivory gown
The lady
The mystery

Curls cascaded
Golden
Faded

Pieces of mirror
Revealed the warrior
Lancelot

Mystery?

The Lady of Shalott.

Emily Parker (13)
Balcarras School

Night Fright

The wind is howling, a storm is brewing,
And we are stuck out at sea.
The ship is a mess and there's lots to be doing
As we all run around busily.

Now comes the rain beating down on our sails;
We are finding it harder to see.
And just when we need it our ship engine fails;
There are so many jobs now for me.

Then comes the thunder, an ear-splitting sound,
Like that of plates being crashed
And if we survive, will we ever be found,
Or will they just think we have smashed?

Although it is raining our eyes recognise
Vague shapes looming before us.
Now what we can see is enormous in size
We have reason for making a fuss.

The captain shouts orders and we all obey
As the ship swerves round to the right
Before we know it we are out of the way
But we panic throughout the night.

When up comes the sun, the storm is far gone
And we see the results of the night.
The first piece of land we set eyes upon
We will land on with the greatest delight.

Jennie Goodrum (14)
Balcarras School

Kiss Me Goodnight

So, kiss me goodnight.

In the slumber of your kiss,
May I rest my weary eyes
From the brutality of war.

May I tread the paths of Heaven,
In the halcyon haze of memory
That hides me from the reality of this day.

In this slumber deep,
May I walk in your stride
Through the ripened fields of grain.

For in the sweetness of your kiss;
Fields of war are fields of grain
And the brutality of the day has ceased to exist.

So, kiss me goodnight
And, in the slumber of your kiss
Forever hold me tight.

Jasmin Stevens (15)
Balcarras School

About Her Person

(Based on 'The Lady of Shalott' by Alfred Lord Tennyson)

Six pieces of glass, exactly,
Thin pieces of string, wrapped tightly.

A needle sharp,
Broken but dark.

The boat was brown, slashed with a blade,
Her name was carved, deep and proud.

On her finger a prick of blood
In her hair a tangle of thread.

Nobody cares
Yet one knight does stare

The knight's eyes began to water
His lips trembled as her hand he caught

Yet the woman lay still
Like an old, pale stone

No colour had she on her skin
That was everything.

Josh Tyler (14)
Balcarras School

About Her Person

(Based on 'The Lady of Shalott' by Alfred Lord Tennyson)

Her art is her tapestry,
Her identity is the mystery.

Her attire torn,
Her love in mourn.

Her final song,
She sang.

In her hand,
A knife as if a final demand.

Her face in a smile,
Because she did not fail.

Her name
Will
Stay.

Her life no more is watching shadows,
For she is the Lady of Shalott.

For she is the Lady of Shalott.

Laura Dodds (13)
Balcarras School

Gives Me Energy, Makes Me Smile

Hearing the beat of the drums,
Gets me to think of the beat.

Gives me *energy*

Hearing my favourite song,
Urges me to drum along.

Makes me *smile*

Green Day, Foo Fighters, The White Stripes.
Bob Marley, Blink 182 and Nirvana

Give me *energy,* make me *smile*

(Don't want to be an American idiot) all my life,
(Smells like Teen Spirit) when I'm down.
Hearing my favourite drummer inspires me.

Gives me *energy,* makes me *smile*

Playing drums with Gretsch and Zildjian,
Rods of Music in my hands.
The rhythm through my body

Gives me *energy,* makes me *smile.*

Robin Smith (13)
Balcarras School

Obsession

Obsessive thoughts still taint me slightly,
As I try to walk away from your memory
Leave you behind
Move on.
I am doing this to save who I am.
I wish you could understand
My reasons for cutting you
Forever out of my life.

Do you not see?

My visions are clouded, and I no longer
Like 'other' boys.
I only see you
And it isn't fair, it isn't normal.
This is why I am pushing you away
And running.

The definition of obsession is:

*Compulsive preoccupation with a fixed idea or
an unwanted feeling or emotion,
often accompanied by symptoms of anxiety.*

Alex Eastman (15)
Balcarras School

About Her Person

(Based on 'The Lady of Shalott' by Alfred Lord Tennyson)

All alone
depressed
she sits
weaving
watching
boredom
trapped

one step
two steps
she has no choice
she hears the voice
lived the life she lived for
forgot the man she longed for
happiness

a knife
a life
a dream
alone
free.

Sophie Bruce-Watt (13)
Balcarras School

About Her Person

(Based on 'The Lady of Shalott' by Alfred Lord Tennyson)

A lonely tower, dark and old,
Inside a lady weaves alone.
A mirror, shadows,
A life it showed.

Flowers, friends, the river blue,
No past, no future, no knight to be true.
Hit the limit, looked, unlocked,
Saw the world, mirror cracked.

A breath of fresh air,
Felt the curse down on her.
Wrote her name on the prow,
Sailed far out.

Singing loudly, her final song,
Death upon, she'd never belong.
To Camelot the river brought her,
Past young wed lovers.

Sir Lancelot did see her face,
She, now dead, may rest in peace.
Who can say what risks were taken,
No one knows but that was everything.

Zoe Haden (13)
Balcarras School

Princesses

There once was a princess called Ella,
Who discovered a horrible smella!
She searched up and down,
And all round the grounds,
And found a dead body in the cellar.

There once was a princess called Alice,
Who lived in a beautiful palace.
She slept all day long,
With a lullaby song.
Then drank some more wine from a chalice.

There once was a princess called Leah,
Who sat in a tree drinking beer.
She fell from the tree,
And broke her knee,
And spilt all the beer in her ear.

There once was a princess called Elaine,
Who was always considered a pain.
At home she was sad,
At school she was bad,
So her school teachers gave her the cane.

Rachael Bromelow (15)
Balcarras School

Night-Time

Creepy creatures, witches and a goblin,
Centaurs, robbers, the list is never-ending.
Dark is coming and Hell is here
Wrapping the world with a powerful sleep,
Reaching, grabbing, tearing at me.
So afraid I dare not look up
Hiding my face amongst new books
From all those nasties - mythical and true.
Worried out of my mind, not that I knew
That there were no witches and a goblin,
Centaurs, robbers, the list is never-ending
All in my mind and none of it true.

I'd made them up and they seemed so real
Quietly watching for their three-course meal
The witches with their long, black gowns,
Transparent faces, feet not touching the ground.
The goblins - short and with beards
And small red hats over their small pink ears.

I never saw anyone but just in case,
I never looked up and I hid my face.

Sally White (11)
Balcarras School

Who Am I?

As I walk down the street,
        People stare.
Their eyes wide with disgust,
        And hatred.
It's because I'm different.

Do any of them know me?
        No.
Have I done anything to them?
        Never.
It's because I'm different.

The words they mutter,
The knife they stick in me.
They make me ashamed
Of who I am.

        Who am I?
In their eyes:
        The Stick Man
In mine:
        Just me.

Annie Bryson (15)
Balcarras School

The Day I Won The Lottery

It was great, it was fab, I was over the moon,
Everyone said it was rather too soon.
But oh no, the things I could buy,
Shoes, bags and DKNY.
Billabong, Quiksilver, Topshop too,
The shopping sprees, cars, everything new,
Now we could afford it we'd never be sad,
Wc could give some to charity, I'm sure they'd be glad,
Summer would be bliss, the holidays fab,
In winter we'd be cosy, ordering a cab.

But people would want to be my friend,
Just for the money, for loans and a lend.
Cheapskates and frauds would start appearing,
Especially when Saturday night was nearing.
How could I tell who was honest and true?
How could I spot them, what could I do?
Lie detector, shifty eyes, fickle and flighty,
All that money made me feel high and mighty.
But wait a minute, what's gone on?
Everything has just gone wrong.
Oh my goodness, count the cost,
I looked in my purse and my ticket was lost!

Felicia Tennant (11)
Balcarras School

kiss100.com.ode

Oh, the fabulous Kisstory,
Featuring Pink to Cassidy,
And 50 Cent among others,
Not appealing to our mothers.
The 'do', clothes, ice, rims and the bling,
Make the stars' wallets go 'k-ching'.
Cruising along Sunset Melrose,
Or Hollywood, it's all a pose.

The charts with the Hollywood stars,
Spending a lifetime in the bars,
VIP entries into clubs,
Don't bother with those small-town pubs.
The river, caviar, and Cristowe,
Kiss100.com tells how.
If your heart yearns for all of this,
All you gotta do is watch 'Kiss'!

The various charts like Smooth Grooves,
Banging out the latest tunes.

It is to Kiss that this we owe.
So thank you Kiss for all the music,
This channel, I'll always choose it.

Roxanne Parkins (15)
Balcarras School

Santa's Christmas Journey

It is the night of Christmas Eve
Everyone is asleep
Santa lands his sleigh
And down the chimney he creeps

With a sack on his back
And a cookie in his hand
'This is the life,' he says
Better than any other land

He lays out the presents
And drinks the milk from the tray
Vanishes up the chimney
And returns to his sleigh

He gives the reindeer the nod
To fly to the next town
To give Sarah her doll
And Timmy his clown

He delivers his last
No sign of a tear
Because as he knows
There's always next year.

Carrie Knight (13)
Balcarras School

Tennyson's Lady

(Based on 'The Lady of Shalott' by Alfred Lord Tennyson)

Sway the boat, beneath the willow,
Hear the waters rush below.
  On the bow, standing tall,
    Her last hope, a crucible.

        Reddened lips, and down her cheeks,
          Pale skin, tear-streaked.
            Empty, darkened hollow eyes,
              Staring up at wild skies.

          Winds gust, leaves quiver;
            Twist and turn, down the river.
          Surge the currents, ebb and flow,
        Down the river, down she go.

    And now they see her, drifting by,
Tears linger in her eyes.
They read her name around the prow,
    Their hearts they cross, their heads they bow.

        While in her limp and icy hand,
          One might wonder what they found . . .
            At last, the golden key.

                'Gentle Lord, I come to thee.'

Dominique Gibbons (13)
Balcarras School

Silly Words

Poo,
    Loo.
        Book,
            Cook.
                Mow cow,
                    Bow.

            I know these are silly words
            And it's like they fly around,
            With birds.

        In the sky,

          Up high.

But kids feel so bound
    To boring words, day after day,
        But one day I may
            See poems with silly words
                That fly around, like birds,

        In the sky,

          Up high,

            Bye-bye.

Tim Harrison (15)
Balcarras School

Who Am I?

I have a name, but won't tell you just yet.
I have a story to tell you, to move you
But I don't even know you
Why should I tell you? We haven't even met.
All I can tell you is my looks
I have to warn you,
I'm no Cinderella or Sleeping Beauty
Like you read in the books.

I have brown hair and blue eyes
I'm not rich or poor, I'm average size
The rest is a secret,
I'll tell you but it's supposed to be a surprise.
(Do you know who I am?)
I don't care, I don't give a damn
One day you will find out my name
But creep when you leave.
Quiet, don't shout!

Anon

Jordan Moore (15)
Balcarras School

Good Friends!

When we are together,
Everything is fine,
We laugh and joke, we chase and fight,
But the days always turn out right,
Because we're such good friends.

We have such fun,
Everything is great,
We sing and dance, we play and run,
No matter what, we still have fun,
Because we're such good friends.

Kayleigh Walker (13)
Barnwood Park High School

And She Was Gone

She runs, she walks,
She tries, she tries,
She lifted her face towards the skies.

Some say she wished too hard,
Some say she wished too long,
Some say she spread her arms out wide.

And she was gone.

But I know!

She spread her arms out wide,
As she held on,
For the breaking dawn.

Then she was gone.

The stars are bright,
The wind is cold,
The moon is big and so very bold.

She runs, she walks, she tries, she tries
She lifted her face
Towards the bright, bright skies.

And she was gone.

Emma Mathieson (11)
Barnwood Park High School

The Busy Ants

Ants are scuttling in and out
Around the paving and all about.
Building tunnels that lead to small chambers
Hoping to get out of any dangers.
Digging up sand so soft and fine
Really this nest will be divine.

Carolyn Moser (11)
Barnwood Park High School

Reasons
(Dedicated to Nan)

I think that people walk for a reason.
I think that people talk for a reason.
Why, oh why, do people die? It seems so unfair
But everything has a reason.
You could call it fate, but everything has a reason.

There are reasons to:
Shout,
Laugh,
Dance,
Whisper,
Cry,
Sing.
And even
Fight.

I had a reason to write this poem.

Arianna Clarke (11)
Barnwood Park High School

Floods

The rain came down,
It flooded over into the town
Splash, crash, splash!

Objects floated downstream
It was not very clean
Splash, crash, splash!

Cars hit buildings
As the water came up to the ceiling
Crash, splash, crash!

Everyone started screaming
Which left everyone reeling.
Splash, crash, splash,
Crash!

Faye Partlett (12)
Barnwood Park High School

Typical Secondary

When the teacher leaves the classroom,
Children get out of control.
One typical person starts playing up
And scrunches paper in a ball.
One boff sighs,
But the others pretend they don't hear and just fuss by.
Girls and boys stand on tables,
Messing everywhere up.
But the boff in the corner is *sooo* fed up.
When the teacher comes back,
Everybody sits on their chair,
But the typical person just carries on
And pretends the teacher's not there.
The teacher notices something,
And everybody starts to laugh.
It says on the whiteboard
that Mr Cooper never takes a bath!

Serin Coskun (12)
Barnwood Park High School

A Poem For The Young

In a long, long time,
When we all grow old,
Lots of us may be bald,
We'll be much wiser than ever before,
We'll be old and grey for evermore,
We'll lose our hair, and our teeth,
But here's the thing to cause you grief,
You'll lose sense of fashion, music and style,
You may be lonely for a while,
But soon you'll find some good old friends,
And I mean old, and round the bend!

Amber Holdaway-Brown (12)
Barnwood Park High School

Lost And Forgotten

Scream,
Shout,
Swear,
Stamp,
No one even cares.

Wail,
Whine,
Whimper,
Wonder,
No one gives a damn.

Clatter,
Cry,
Collapse,
Crash,
No one even notices.

Call,
Whisper,
Stop.
I've been lost and forgotten.

Carrie Talbot (12)
Barnwood Park High School

Jim

Even though his death was sad,
Jim was still very bad.
I didn't like him anyway,
But I liked what he had to say.
Pronto was a naughty beast,
He'd do anything for a feast.
No more tea, cakes or jam,
They were all given to his mum, Pam.
Their son is dead,
Pronto should be dead instead!
That's what his mum said.

Kirsty Swinford (12)
Barnwood Park High School

Creatures

Elephants go like this and that,
they're terribly big and terribly fat,
they have no fingers, they have no toes,
but goodness gracious, what a long nose!

Snakes slither side to side
hissing to the left and hissing to the right
camouflaging in the deep, deep sand
a creature you don't want to handle by hand.

Fish swimming left and swimming right,
fishermen give them a terrible fright.
Always making an effort to go upstream
to hide from predators so as not to be seen.

Spiders creeping and crawling round and round,
getting in corners so they can't be found,
catching flies in their lovely silk webs,
sleeping silently in their tiny, little beds.

Megan McMurray (11)
Barnwood Park High School

Gentle Twist

You are the sunlight by which I shine
A glow in a foggy mist
All of yours and all of mine
Giving life a gentle twist

I am the water for you to drink
The timber for you to build
I think you are the missing link
Emptiness has now been filled

You are the muscle of my strength
I am the rock on which you lean
This love of ours has no length
The end is unforeseen.

Katriona Stuart (13)
Barnwood Park High School

Nan's Pyjamas
(A true story)

I'll write you a poem, that'll make you laugh.
It's Saturday morning, Nan's having a bath.

The silence is shattered, the phone starts to ring,
she jumps out of the bath, she's not wearing a thing.

She runs down the stairs, to answer that phone
and after she's had a good natter and a moan,

she runs back upstairs, and here's where you laugh,
her pyjamas are floating around in the bath.

How did they get there? She just isn't sure.
The last time she saw them, they were laid on the floor.

The moral of the story, when answering the phone,
is never to leave your pyjamas alone.

Yvonne Jebb (12)
Barnwood Park High School

City Jungle

Sun blazes town.
People storm through frustrated crowds,
unaware of others.
Rubbish sizzles into thin air.
Motorbikes whiz past
until their thirsty engines come to a halt
as the traffic lights turn
from glowing green to ruby red.
Crabby cats raid for shade,
lounging and scrounging
for scraps where they can.
Blistering buildings stand tall.
Roads turn into bubbling lakes of tarmac
and shops and pavements shimmer
in the hazy, hot atmosphere.

Sarah Bebbington (12)
Barnwood Park High School

My Shadow

Wherever I walk, it walks too,
It follows me everywhere,
When I jump, skip or run, it does the same as me.

If I jump then it does a jump,
But it always stays on the ground,
It can do everything I can do
But it cannot make a sound.

Most days it comes out to play,
But never when it's cloudy,
I don't know why,
But it never does. *Never!*

When the sky starts to get dark,
My shadow starts to fade,
Then suddenly when the sky is pitch-black,
My shadow is gone until the next day.

Nicola Barton (11)
Barnwood Park High School

Cats

Some cats are fat and some cats are skinny,
One cat that I know is even called Minnie,
Sometimes when you stroke her you get a handful of fur,
You know when she likes that because she will purr,
If she's not in the mood for playing she may possibly scratch,
And she likes stalking birds which she tries to catch,
A game Minnie loves is chasing her tail,
The funniest thing is that she always fails,
Minnie's breed is a Persian blue,
And maybe one day you will own a cat like her too!

Lucy Trotman (13)
Barnwood Park High School

Sharks

Sharks are really scary,
When we swim we are wary,
No wonder we're frightened,
If we think one's behind us,
'Cause sharks are really scary.

Their big, gnashing jaws,
Cause riots and wars,
Their skin (if you've been close enough) is soft
It feels really cold,
'They're cold-blooded animals,' I was told.

I think to be,
A shark, you see,
Is not very easy,
Because they're sleazy
And nobody likes them at all!

Take my advice,
Just be nice,
When face to face with a shark,
No need to beware,
It'll sense you are scared,
But stay out of the way in the dark!

Georgia Brightmore (12)
Barnwood Park High School

I Wish

I wish I were a millionaire
I wish it could be true
But what I have is what I need
    All I need is you.

I wish I could have all I want
I wish it could be true
But what I have is what I need
    I don't need anything but you.

Stephanie Whalley (12)
Churchdown School

I See

Through the lens I see,
People all colours and shades,
Happy, smiling, sad, starving and dead

I see colours of sunshine,
Colours of nature, rainbows, sea and mountains

I see cities, skyscrapers,
Roads, cars and lorries, under and through

I see old and wise
Young and fresh, middle-aged and tired

I see furry and ferocious
Slimy and slithery
Under the sea in the air

I see back streets and buses
Trains and travellers
Subways and monorails, tickets and passes

I see saris and masks
Hats, coats, uniforms and overalls

I see waterfalls and oceans
Deserts and glaciers, jungle, green rainforest

I see through my camera lens.

Howard Colin (13)
Churchdown School

School

I go to school in the morning.
I go on the bus today.
I go into class and it is very boring.
At the end of the day I shout, 'Hooray, hooray!'

Richard Aunger (12)
Churchdown School

The Sad Story Of Lefty And Ted

There were two crooks called Lefty and Ted
Who had to steal for their daily bread
But now they're dead or so they said
But I still think they're alive

They sobbed for bread, pleaded for money
They got no money, stole some honey
But now they're dead or so they said
But I still think they're alive

They stole from the rich, gave to the poor
They kept some themselves and went for more
But now they're dead or so they said
But I still think they're alive

One day they planned to rob the bank
The other side of the riverbank
But now they're dead or so they said
But I still think they're alive

They dug all day and dug all night
They dug until morn's first light
But now they're dead or so they said
But I still think they're alive

The bank came tumbling down on them
The whole wide world caved in on them
But now they're dead or so they said
But I still think they're alive

And now the moral, crime never pays
You'd be best take note of this worthy phrase
But now they're dead or so they said
But I still think they're alive.

Sean Baker (13)
Churchdown School

Homeless People

I am a homeless person,
And some people need to learn some
Facts about the homeless,
And how they became thus.

One of the facts,
Is because they don't pay tax;
Or just aren't able to get a job,
And all they do is sit and sob.
When they can't get a job,
They don't get money,
And can't pay their bills.
They lose their home,
And can't find another.
Some carry on trying to find a job,
And some don't give a sod.
The ones who don't give a sod,
End up begging and sleeping more roughly.

There are also the ones, who have fights at home,
And end up leaving home.
Then most of them can't find another home,
And the DSS won't give them a job,
Because they moved out of their home,
By their own free will.
And that is how I became homeless too.

And it sometimes makes me feel ill,
The way people turn their noses up at us,
As if we shouldn't be here in this world.

Maria-Eléna Ridgway (13)
Churchdown School

Insanity

I'm wishing on a star for one of those days,
When you have everything you wanted,
Not one when you feel haunted.
I've had so many of them recently,
It feels so much different than sanity,
You can't choose what to do,
It gets chosen for you.
That's why I'm wishing on a star,
So I can get that one little *'ting'*,
So my wish becomes true which is to bar
Everything that stands in my way,
And that I can get out of this insanity today.
What I'm really wishing for,
Is to get over this wall which is ten feet tall,
But I'm only five foot seven,
How am I supposed to reach up to Heaven?
But with such a small height,
I have found a way,
And that is to wish upon a star,
And to wish I was dead to float out of this place,
So I can finally face,
The beautiful feeling that you know you're not crazy,
And that you don't have a care about life.
I found that life isn't reality,
When everyone thought I was insane,
Everything seemed so plain,
And so I want to go to the real reality,
That is called Heaven,
And holds no morality.

Sam Cooper (14)
Churchdown School

Homelessness

I'm sitting in a doorway
Freezing, hungry and no money
I tried dossing
But nobody cared

To passers-by I'm invisible
To shopkeepers I'm a nuisance
I tried to get into the Shelter
But nobody cared

Passers-by say,
'Find some work, you scrounger'
I tried the Job Centre
But nobody cared

I haven't got a job, I have no money
And I haven't got any family
I'm still homeless
And still nobody cares.

Bronwen Scales (12)
Churchdown School

New School

Welcome to Churchdown, you'll fit in
You definitely won't be put in the bin
I have come from Year 6, big fish, small pond
I'm now Year 7, small fish, big sea
At first I was frightened no one knew me,

With my new friends we're as happy as can be!

School is fun, school is great,
I can't wait to get to Year 8.

Martyn Edward Adamson (11)
Churchdown School

My Colourful World

If only the sky was pink
If only grass was red
If only the people would think
Then not as many would be dead.
If only the trees were white
If only the sea was green
Maybe the world would be alright
If the people would stop being mean.
If only the fish were yellow
If only the birds were teal
Maybe the people would be more mellow
Maybe everyone could have a meal.
If only the moon was gold
If only the sun was beige
If only the people stopped being so cold
Then we'd stop all this rage.
If only the cities were rosy
If only the houses were blue
If we want our world to be cosy
It's down to me and you!

Charlotte Lewis (12)
Churchdown School

Shopping

So many shops, so little time.
Each one is special to me.
I treasure them and make them mine.
I look forward to Saturdays with glee.

It's only money I need.
Some people think it's greed.
I love to look and not just buy.
New clothes just to try but then buy.

Sophie Davis (11)
Churchdown School

Shopping At 10am

Oh my God, it's 10am,
It's time for me to go shopping again,
Buy some make-up, buy some hair,
Just make sure people don't stare.

£50, spend, spend, spend,
Oh my God, I'm nearly there,
It's time to get fair,
Hello Ami, hello Megs,
Are you ready to hit the shops?
If not, I'll call the cops.

The skirt is black,
The top is blue,
They are so dry colours,
But the pink will make the boys go wink, wink,
So take what I think,
And choose the pink,
And don't be dressed in dry colours.

Chantelle Ali (11)
Churchdown School

Why?

Why, why must we fight war?
Why, why can't we live in peace?
Why, why should men be sent to die?
Why, why do people get sent away from home?

Why, why must children get involved?
Why, why should women get involved?
Why, why can't we get on with each other?
Why, why do we have to pay the price?

Why?

Tom Allen (11)
Churchdown School

My Death Poem

Skeletons roam
through the night and give
everyone a big fright.
I woke up one night and
what I saw was not a nice sight.
A vampire stuck his teeth
into my neck and it felt
like a pigeon's peck!

Along came a mummy
and sucked up all the blood.
Along came a troll and
nearly turned me into
a sausage roll.

Jodie Louise Witts (11)
Churchdown School

Hidden Cries

I sit here just looking a mess,
In a doorway I am here to sleep and rest,
The space I take up is just wasteful,
No one cares, no one is sorrowful.

It's dark and I can feel the coldness,
My fingers are numb and I'm too effortless,
Children walk past, their stomachs full,
All I can do is scavenge food and be hopeful.

The people that walk past are thoughtless,
I'm sure that they think I'm a pest,
I ask the questions how and why,
But all I do is sit and silently cry.

Emily Hyett (12)
Churchdown School

Homeless

Shelter
Got nowhere to spend the night?
Go to this place, it's free alright
Come on mate I'm not gonna bite.

So I took him in and he sat down.
I grabbed my cat Sopho and put him outside
And then when he wasn't looking I got him
Around the neck really tight.

Then I saw another one begging for some money,
I told him, 'I'll take ya for the day.'
So he came to my place and stroked the cat
And I got him, hooray!

Link
Street life is hard and tough
I don't know what to do, go back to Vince
No way, man
I'd rather stay with Ginger

If you have a bad home life think twice about being homeless
You don't get anything to eat
You'll never stay tidy or neat
All you'll do is smell and get in the way.

Ryan Lowe (12)
Churchdown School

Being Homeless

When you're homeless, you're fighting a losing battle;
You feel like there's no need to survive.
You start to smoke, drink and take drugs,
You know you're gonna die but you feel no pain.
The cigarette smoke clouds your vision.
One minute you're sat by a door,
Then *boom,* you're gone, alive no more!

Samantha Reed (12)
Churchdown School

Homeless

Out alone in the cold,
All hairy and very old,
Nobody around to care,
Distasteful looks everywhere.

Hungry, tired, cold and scared,
All my clothes are in tatters and tears,
Begging for money, only 50p,
Just enough for a cup of tea.

Wishing to turn my life around,
As I'm sat here on hard ground,
Dreaming of a warm, cosy home,
But it's just a dream, I'm all
                              Alone!

Emily Trigg (12)
Churchdown School

Homeless

I left home at 12,
And now I'm 18,
And I'm not worth a place on Earth.

I did have a friend,
But now he's gone,
And I am all alone in this cruel world.

I've earned no money,
For the last two days,
I think I will go somewhere else.

I am back at home,
And all is forgot,
After all I am 18, and I am worth a place on Earth.

Sam Myatt (12)
Churchdown School

Shelter

Shelter's my name
Killing clients is my game,
I have three dead people under my floorboards
Which is the perfect place just for them

I have a cat
It's called Sapho,
It's a manky thing,
But let's forget about him!

I used to be in the army,
And nobody could harm me.
I will act like a ninja
And kill Ginger

My next client will be Link
He must be killed.
He's a homeless beggar,
And no one will miss him.

Ross Goodhall (12)
Churchdown School

Loneliness

Hello?
There's no reply.
Is anyone there?
I know someone's there, I can see you, so why don't you talk to me?
'Hello,' I say as someone passes by . . .
But no one sees me . . .
Nothing . . . no recognition, nothing . . .
No one sees me, sitting here . . .
Why don't they talk to me? Why are they avoiding me?
Don't ask me why, they just do . . .
Ask them . . . why they're ignoring me?
They don't realise I'm watching them walk by.

Gareth Jones (12)
Churchdown School

The Hunter And The Hunted

Creeping silently through the dense forest
Deadly and invisible, the tiger is top
A blur that blends into the forest foliage
The deer is calm and relaxed, happy as can be
Unaware of the danger that lurks behind
About to pounce, the tiger is ready
He leaps and . . .
Bang!
The deer runs off scared but safe
But the tiger is less lucky
A strange pale figure emerges casting a dark shadow upon the tiger
It is man,
The killer,
The hunter is the hunted!

Andy Knight (13)
Churchdown School

Homeless

People homeless on the streets
Looking tired, nothing to eat
Lonely, sad, missing home,
No one cares
No one stops
Getting colder every day
Find a doorway,
Find a box
This is home
This is my lot!

Sophie Grimes (12)
Churchdown School

Fish

My poem is all about fish,
Swimming and cooked in a dish.
Keep them in a tank as pets,
Or go catch them in nets.
I like it in fisherman's bake
But not when made into fishcake.
It's quite calming to watch them swim
Back and forth with a waggling tail fin.
Eat it cold or eat it hot
From a can or fresh in a pot.
Sat on a bank with a rod and bait,
For a bite I sit and wait.
Sushi, raw fish sounds yuk,
Think if Mum gave me that I would chuck.
I don't always manage a bite,
Sometimes they put up a fight.
So you see I do like fish,
Either swimming or cooked in a dish.

Ashley Mott (12)
Churchdown School

Pets

I want a new pet
Wonder what it will be
We'll have to wait and see.

It could be a dog, cat or hamster,
They are a bit boring
It could be an elephant that never stops snoring!

I've looked in every book and pet shop
There's lots of choice, I like the bunny that hops!
Maybe I'll just keep my giraffe
At least it makes me laugh.

Ramon Thomas (12)
Churchdown School

Shopping

Saturday morning, shopping time,
Got to make sure I don't cross the line,
'£50, thank you Mum,
Sorry Mum, you can't come.'
'Hello Megan, hello Chan,
It's time to go and call for Dan!'
We've hit the shops, it's shopping time,
Let's go OTT and cross the line.
A row of pink, a row of blue,
'I think the yellow one would go with you.'
'That will be £15 please.'
Oh look, there's a pattern on the knees.
Jumper, jacket, jeans, I feel like a jacket potato
With butter and beans.
I want some new shoes,
'Hey, have you heard the good news?
The good news is I'm buying new shoes!'
'That's it, now I'm going home,
I'll leave you guys alone.'

Ami Ward (11)
Churchdown School

Night

Night is a huge, black blanket,
Where millions of stars glisten
In the cold empty air.

Night is a huge, black blanket,
Where owls twitter to each other
As they look for their prey.

Night is a huge, black blanket,
Where the moon waits
Until morning comes.

Stuart Stephenson (13)
Churchdown School

My Mates

I have really fun mates,
and our relationship never breaks
because we're too much of a kind.

We're always together,
never mind the weather,
this group will never break,
no matter what it takes,
because we're too strong,
to let these long years go disappearing by.

This bond's been going strong for ages
I could write for pages and pages.
But I gotta go now,
I'll see you somehow.
I'm going to be with my mates!

Tiffany Lowery (14)
Churchdown School

If Only . . .

If only money grew on trees,
If only I was the Queen,
If only I went on lots of shopping sprees,
If only everything was green.

If only we lived forever,
If only our wishes came true,
If only I could make people feel better,
If only I was you.

If only we were all treated the same
For our size, looks and colour,
If only when someone hated you,
You loved them like no other.

Chevez Smith (12)
Churchdown School

I Look Into The Sky!

I look into the sky and what do I see?
A funny cloud looking at me.
Its tummy so fat, its beak so pointy.
Its yellow body which is fluffy and soft.
What in the world am I looking at?
It's a yellow duck, a yellow duck I see.

I look into the sky and what do I see?
A funny cloud looking at me.
Its face so wobbly, its eyes so dark.
Its body so see-through and floating.
What in the world am I looking at?
It's a wobbly ghost, a wobbly ghost, I see.

Suzanna Richards (12)
Churchdown School

New School

Big, bold, bright rooms
Lots of strange faces
Large shadows loom
Children running at fast paces.

Different teachers speaking
New lessons to be learnt
Some classrooms even leaking
Cakes and bread that could be burnt.

Lining up in the cold
Children rushing up and down
Standing straight, up and bold
Without a grin or a frown.

Holly Reynolds (11)
Churchdown School

Too Dark To See

It's too dark to see
I'm trapped in the night
With no light shining
I'm lost. It's so cold
I can feel the ice on my face.
A shiver runs down my spine.
Strange sounds surrounding me.
It's deserted. No one to help me.
The shivers rattle my bones.
Maybe it's all a dream
but it's still too dark to see.

Nick Pugh (12)
Churchdown School

My Rabbit

My rabbit is called Toffee
he likes to jump around.
He is the colour of coffee
and sometimes can't be found.
He has long droopy ears
and a great big fluffy tail.
He likes to munch on carrots
and eats hundreds without fail.

Lee Russell (11)
Churchdown School

Chess

C hess is a challenging game
H ard to understand
E ventually you learn how the pieces move
S uccess and it's checkmate!
S mart move.

Sean Mobley (11)
Churchdown School

Diggin' 'Em Holes

Five foot deep and five foot wide.
Eight of us will cram inside.
Beads of sweat run down my head.
Keep on diggin' till we're free or dead!

A flash of yellow or is it gold?
The thought of it makes us chill with cold.
Their teeth are black and tongues of white.
It only takes one poisonous bite.

With fear and dread we start to dig,
And all because he stole that pig.
'Camp Green Lake,' the judge, he said,
'Keep on diggin' till we're free or dead.'

Billy Poulter (12)
Churchdown School

My Special Day

It was very windy
I was about to walk in

I jumped, I caught
I fell back to the hard floor

I could only smile
I threw the red-leathered ball

Into the blue sky
That was the end of my day

I will never forget
That really special day
The game was cricket.

Joe Lawrence (13)
Churchdown School

If Only . . .

If only I could have all the time I want,
I would be able to do anything at any time.

If only I could fly across blue and black skies,
I could see lands of green and yellow.

If only people would never bully each other,
I would make this change.

If only everyone would respect each other
And not think that they are better than everyone else,
I could make things different.

If only there were powers,
I would make the world a better place.

Katie Evans (11)
Churchdown School

Nature

Looking up to the sky so blue
No clouds, only two.

Smelling the flowers so colourful and bright
They were the colours of just red and white.

Watching a plane fly over my head
Looking up now, I just want to be dead

Then I fell back
And a bee flew by
Then I saw now
I just want to cry.

Nicole Lewis (12)
Churchdown School

Baby Aimee

Her eyes are as blue as the sea,
She really is special to me,
She comes with a smile,
But it took her a while,
She really is special to me.

She makes me so happy,
She wears a nappy,
Her hair is so long,
She is so strong,
She really is special to me.

Louise Lewin (12)
Churchdown School

Kittens

My kittens wake up in the morning
Like a baby and eat like a monster

They walk round like explorers
When they are out they run like the wind
And do not stop like a never-ending tornado

They play like sisters and fight to learn to hunt
But do not hit and are friends for life

Edward Durrant (13)
Churchdown School

Sport

Sport is the best thing in the world to me.
Football is my favourite sport.
You have to run fast and be flexible too.
But rugby is a tough game.
You need to be strong for that!

Daniel Marks (11)
Churchdown School

Friends

I have a friend called Chev
I have a friend called Charlie
I have a friend called Phil
But none of them are equal to Steph

She's the best friend in the world
Steph's someone you can really trust
What would I do without my dear friend Bush?
Now that's her nickname, Bush
It's from her bushy eyebrows

She's always there
And thanks, I really care
I don't care what she looks like
Or that she doesn't have a bike
She's like a sister to me
But my real sister looks like a flea

So this really is just a special thanks
For all the things you've had to put up with
I don't know what I would do without you
Cos through the good and through the bad
You were there
That shows you care
So thanks, you big, old bear.

Kimberley Iliffe (12)
Churchdown School

If Only

If only I had all the money in the world then I would help everyone.
If only I was clever, I would get a really good job.
If only people would stop killing then they wouldn't be extinct.
If only we could have world peace then there would be no murders.
If only there was no pollution then no one would get poisoned.
If only we had enough supplies to keep all of us alive.
But this is the way the world is and this is the way I am.

Sam Large (12)
Churchdown School

Sports

Football is great,
It's really cool,
I play for a football team,
For Churchdown School.

Golf is wicked,
It's really fab,
It's better than maths,
Or working in a lab.

I really like snooker,
The club I've joined is great,
I pot all the balls,
And beat my mate.

Swimming is fun,
Splash, splash,
Up and down the pool,
I go like a flash.

Rugby, I'm not too sure,
I haven't played it before,
If I do I'll score,
Which will make me play it more.

Jake O'Malley (11)
Churchdown School

Morning

Ring, ring, went my clock
I tried to get dressed but couldn't find my sock,
I ran downstairs to get my breakie,
But then I realised I wasn't yet ready,
I grabbed my bag, got in the car,
I thought to myself, *I am a star,*
My mum opened the door, 'You fool,' she said.
'There is no school!'

Jordan Kline (12)
Churchdown School

My Baby Cousin

His eyes are as blue as Heaven,
They shine like the stars,
His blond hair shines like the sun,
With him you're sure to have fun.
He really is special!

He's happy and cheerful,
His smile lights the room,
He's sure to come with a bang!
He's hopeful and will go far.
He really is a little star!

Debbie Hayes (12)
Churchdown School

The Creature

There once was a creature
Who lived in a shell
He loved his little home
Which he knew so well.
He never ever left it
In fear of creatures big
So he never got eaten or bit!

Haydon King (11)
Churchdown School

Resources

If only, if only the last leaf falls
If only, if only the last fish dies
If only, if only the farmyard leaves
If only, if only the last shop closes
If only, if only the last flower dies
If only, if only the last water droplet dries
Then people would realise money isn't anything.

Kyle Coe (12)
Churchdown School

The Match

I walk to the rugby ground
I am feeling excited
I am going to watch my favourite team play
I find my friends and we go to stand in our usual spot
The teams come out and begin to warm up
The crowd starts to cheer.

The teams get ready for kick-off
The captain kicks the ball and the crowd cheers
As the ball flies up into the air
Oh no, he drops the ball and loses the ball to the other team!
A fierce tackle and we get the ball back.

Hooray, we've won!
The crowd cheers
The noise fills the stadium
I feel glad because my favourite team played brilliantly
We walk home in the rain
But I don't mind because we won!

Matthew Etchells (12)
Churchdown School

Football

Football is my game
Football is my aim
I can use both feet
To score a goal
I can kick the ball up high
Almost to the sky
I can kick the ball left or right
Depending on the night.

Football is my goal in life.

Daniel Weir (11)
Churchdown School

Footy!

I love it!
I can't stop thinking about it!
I can't stop playing it!
I can't live without it!
If I'm not playing it I'm thinking about it!
Hopefully I'm going to play for Chelsea one day!
Nothing can stop me from playing it!

Liam Shotbolt (11)
Churchdown School

Food

I love food it is so yummy
And I like it in my tummy
Any type, anywhere
As long as it is not healthy
I don't care
I would eat, eat, eat.

Bradley Hall (11)
Churchdown School

The Turtle

I knew a turtle that hid in its shell,
Just because it couldn't yell,

I tried and tried,
But was not satisfied,

Because I couldn't make the turtle yell.

Ross Wheeler (12)
Churchdown School

Love

Everyone argues with me
Everyone shouts at me
Nobody has a kind word for me
All I need is love.

I need shelter
I need hope
I need family and friends who care
All I need is love.

I am scared
I am frightened
Because I am all alone
All I need is love.

I smoke
I cry
I don't know what to do
All I need is love.

I don't want much
But my life is important
I only can hope
Someone is listening to me.

All I need is love.
All I need is love.
All I need is love.
All I need is love.

Suzanne Murray (14)
Churchdown School

Fire

F ire is hot
I t burns rapidly
R ed-raw or not
E ither way, it's still hot.

Shane Trigg (12)
Churchdown School

Darkness

I was walking into sheer darkness, nothing looked the same.
The noises screeching, screaming as the dead of night came.
Imagine how strange I felt, nothing looked the same.
I sprinted into the shop and grabbed what I needed.
I walked to the counter, when I heard heavy breathing beside me.
I turned to have a look, but no one was there.

I edged nearer the door and out into the night
Still the heavy breathing giving me a fright.
I ran into the dark, trying to find my way.
My heart was pounding, my fear running away.
I fumbled with my key in the lock and at last was safely
                                        through the door.
In the light of my home I realised that the heavy breathing was me!

Samuel Wheeler (11)
Churchdown School

Wild Animals

W eeping whales swimming through the sea
 I rritable ibex looking at you and me
L icking lizards creeping around
D iving dolphins making a chattering sound

A nnoying anteaters sniffing the ground
N asty newts swimming around
 I maginable iguanas licking the air
M ischievous monkeys, they just stare
A gonising apes swing away
L arge lions they just lay
S parkling starfish float away.

Jade Stacey (11)
Churchdown School

School, School, School

School, school, school
Up at 7 and out at 3
Sometimes fun, sometimes boring
But we all have to do it to get a job we like.

School, school, school
They make us write for hours on end!
How boring is that?
But we all have to do it to get a job we like.

School, school, school
They give you homework, what is up with that?
Just taking up your free time
But we all have to do it to get a job we like.

School, school, school
I know you're up at 7
I know it is boring too
Making you write for hours on end
And to top it all up, homework as well
But we all have to do it to get a job we like.

Siobhan How (13)
Churchdown School

Urban

Fumes and gases in the sky,
Fields and hills say goodbye.

A world in itself hides within,
Amongst the clamour, racket and din.

Hustle and bustle, on the roads,
Pedestrians ignoring the Green Cross Code.

Finally when the noise goes down the drain,
The sun comes up and it starts again.

George Richards (11)
Churchdown School

In School

I CT

N ouns

S ubjects

C onfidence

H elping

O pportunity

O rganiser

L essons.

Samantha Cooper (11)
Churchdown School

My Sister Smelly!

My sister Smelly
put deodorant in her welly,
Her farts are stinky,
you can smell them in Helsinki!
If you put them in a jet pack,
you can get to Iraq!

Jenny Humphris (11)
Churchdown School

What Is A Bully?

A bully is someone who is mean.
A bully takes your lunch money.
A bully pushes you around.
A bully makes you cry.
Are you a bully?

Harry Lewis (13)
Churchdown School

The Tadpole

I'm a little tadpole,
Swimming around the pond,
Sometimes me and my brothers,
Act like James Bond.

Swimming, jiggling, wiggling,
Dancing round and round,
As I get some legs,
I can then pound around.

I'm all grown up now,
I've turned into a frog,
But guess what comes sometimes?
I think it's called a dog.

Jumping, leaping, pounding,
On my lily pad,
No one to share life with,
Oh how sad . . .

Zoe Hitchen (13)
Churchdown School

My Nan

My nan is my friend,
She's one of a kind,
She's always there to listen and share,
She makes me laugh when she sings loud in church,
My nan makes great cakes and shares them with mates,
She loves to watch me dance whenever she can,
My nan is from Wales and tells lots of tales of what it was like
to grow up in Wales,
She's proud of me and as you can see
I love my nan,
As much as I can.

Bethan Morgan (13)
Churchdown School

My Dreams

My dreams are happening all the time,
even when I'm awake.
I dream of the latest super-fast cars,
the type that are impossible to make.

I dream of being the smartest and the fastest.
The best there ever was,
but never to know why or because.

Adam Leach (13)
Churchdown School

Whatever Next?

Bang!   The wind slammed the door shut,
Pop!   Went the noise of the Coke bottle opening,
Whistle!   Went the wind in the breeze,
Brum!   Went the motorbike,
Clang!   Went the glasses as they met together,
Tick-tock! Went the old grandfather clock.

Louis Fawl (11)
Churchdown School

My School Bag

Every morning I pack my schoolbooks in my bag.
My calculator, my pens, I can't forget.
I need these for my maths and art.
My PE kit goes in ready for my football,
Along with my coat, a little creased and not that smart.
My lunch box is last to be packed.
It is full of nice goodies waiting to be unwrapped.

Thanks Mum for packing my bag!

Shane Deeley (11)
Churchdown School

Violence

There's too much violence
In the world today,
People being killed
For reasons no one will say.
Horrifying scenes
That are very gory,
People killing each other
For power, money and glory.
There are people starving
And people dying,
Being shot because of their religion
And children who are crying.
Why do we live in a world like this?
Some people have explanations
Others do not,
Kids waking up at night
Because they hear a gunshot.
There's no going back now
It's just too late,
A world full of anger
A world full of hate.
But it is all our fault,
We made the world this way
With people getting killed
For reasons no one will say.

Louisa Gorman (13)
Churchdown School

School - Haiku

It's hard at my school,
All these tests crowd through my head,
And bore me to death.

Sam Hancock (13)
Churchdown School

The First Day

I woke up feeling strange,
my mind was in a daze.
I didn't want to do anything,
but stay in bed.
I said bye to my mum
and off I went,
uncomfortable in my new clothes.
Just before I reached the bus stop
it hit me like a ton of bricks,
work, work, work!
I looked around,
many looked the same as me.
We finally reached our destination,
the sign on the building said,
'Welcome to Churchdown School.'

George Evans (11)
Churchdown School

My Mates Poem

Becky, Zoë, Millie, Sam,
We're all a part of a little gang,
We play around all together,
All the way through the summer,
We have some fun and play some games,
Especially when it's dull and rains,
Even when we had sad times
We have each other on our minds,
It just goes to show,
We're really good friends,
And anything that happens,
Would go to mends.

Becky Nash (13)
Churchdown School

Always In Trouble

Always in trouble with the cops.
Never has a case been dropped.
Shoplifting, fighting, that is all.
Oh yeah there was the graffiti on the neighbour's wall.
Always in a scrap or fight.
Does not come home at night.
Common assault with a hammer.
Now he's in the slammer.
If he doesn't change his evil ways,
He'll be there for the rest of his days.

Jack Christmas (11)
Churchdown School

Stalling

S low down and take your time, don't rush.
T hink what else you've got to do first.
A lways something to stall about,
L aughing about winding your parents up,
L isten to us argue,
I magine what it would be like to do something immediately,
N o, never, not with me,
G etting to bed - it takes so long!

Ryan Deas (11)
Churchdown School

Summer Dreams

We're all going on a summer holiday, summer holiday
where the sun glistens on the warm water,
where the sand is baking hot like a cooker,
and the only shade is under a tropical tree
where dreams come true,
and friendly girls give me big coconuts and juicy fruits.

Dominic Vanstone (13)
Churchdown School

My Sister

My sister is special from beginning to end.
She's my sister and she's my best friend.

She makes me happy when I've been sad,
And helps me out when I've been bad.

She's my inspiration to turn corners in life,
Because I don't want to be as straight as a knife.

When I feel ill, she'll clean my room,
She'll make it gleam like a blossoming bloom.

During the life we've lived, we've been through lots,
We're now in beds but we started in cots.

To my special sister I just want to say,
I love you more, each and every day.

Even though you're my sister, from beginning to end,
You'll always be my best, best friend.

Kelly Whitmore (13)
Churchdown School

The Beautiful Game

Football, football,
Most children's dream
Winning cups for their favourite team.

Cheering and shouting inspires the team,
As every player fulfils the wonderful dream
Premiership, Division 1, 2, or three
Football is always the beautiful game for me!

Football, football,
Most children's dream
Winning cups for their favourite team.

Tom Willetts (11)
Churchdown School

I Can't Find You . . .

I'm walking in my lonely sights
No need to get the frights
I start to run, I feel footsteps coming after me.
I don't look back, I can't see
I can't stop, keep running
It's getting louder, it's drumming
I don't know where I'm heading to.
I need to find you.
I can't find you with someone after me.
I don't look back, I can't see
Help! I trip.
I hear a skip.
I look up behind me.
There's no one there as far as I can see.
I'm still trying to find you
I finally see you
All bright and yellow
All glossy and mellow
It's you, sun,
That's what I've done.
I'm walking in my lonely sights
No need to get the frights.

Bridie Banon (11)
Churchdown School

My Memory Bank Has Been Robbed

My memory bank has been robbed,
All the nice memories are gone,
All that is left is darkness and evil.
My memory bank has been robbed,
My memory is poor again.

Timothy Campbell (11)
Churchdown School

Food

Food is great - I love it all!
Anything you can name
From chocolate to cheese
From meat to wheat
Name any food - I love it!
It tastes so good
Everything apart from

Sprouts!

Adam Brain (12)
Churchdown School

Teachers

Teacher, teacher, why are we wrong?
We work so hard but end up wrong.
You give us work like we know what to do
but end up with detention.

PE, PE, it's so bad, all we do is run, run, run.
PE, PE, why do we do it?
The teacher is not fit, not fit.

Craig Bolton (11)
Churchdown School

My Magic Box
(Inspired by 'Magic Box' by Kit Wright)

My magic box contains wind, rain, snow and all the elements.
I have all the fights, lies and war in my magic box.
My life is in my magic box.
My secrets are hidden, and all my bad dreams.
My magic box is wooden, encrusted with gems, the colour
                                    of the rainbow.

Bethan Petersen (12)
Churchdown School

Why?

Why does it happen?
No one really knows.
Utter confusion.
People fleeing.
Villages destroyed.
Why?
No communication.
Only fighting.
Why?
Babies left alone.
Mothers crying,
Pleading, sighing.
Total despair.
Why?
I don't have the answers.
I just wish I knew why?

Charlotte Smith (11)
Churchdown School

Friendship

F riends are important
R eliable and trustworthy
I n every kind of way
E ach and every day
N ever let you down
D oing things together
S upporting one another
H aving fun along the way
I n our home and at the park
P artying the night away!

Faye Warner (11)
Churchdown School

Friendship

When I wake up in the morning I know we'll still be good friends.
At school we'll play together and play all our favourite games.
Sometimes we'll have some good times, and even bad times.
After school you'll come and call on me and we'll have a
                                        smashing time.
I hope you won't forget my birthday then give me something
                                        I don't like.
I'll remember our special times, even the silliest of them all.
The best times for me have to be playing football, even though
                                        you can't kick at all.
For your birthday I know you like diamonds, but even though
                        sometimes they're unaffordable, I'll give you a hug.
At the end of school we'll go to McDonald's and buy everything
                                        they've got.
When we have a sleepover, I know we'll boogie all night.

Tanya Mutingwende (11)
Churchdown School

Prince Family

P ristine and clean are we
R ight and nice we can be
I ntelligent and perfect we are
N oisy and loud from afar
C alamities around every corner await
E xciting but nail-biting our days unfold

F antastic and funny, we'll make you laugh
A family together, and rarely apart
M ale and female both alike
I nsight into my family you've had
L oveable and adorable
Y es, the Princes are we.

Alice Prince (11)
Churchdown School

Hair

I can be curly or wavy,
Frizzy or straight.
Take too long over me and you might be late.
I need looking after or I could get greasy or split ends.
Shampoo and conditioner are my friends,
I can be blonde, brunette or even pink!
And in addition to what you might think,
In the end I will either fall out or go grey,
So make the most of me, your hair, today!
Tie me up or braid me,
Let me grow long, wild and free.
My long list of possibilities never end,
I am truly your best friend.

Lauren Wilden (13)
Newent Community School

I Thought . . .

I thought we were friends,
But are we not?
I loved you once, but you forgot.

I will be here,
In your time of fear,
To tell you I love you,
That I need you too.

If I go before you do,
I'll go to Heaven and wait for you,
This friendship will last forever.

My eyes have been crying,
My heart has been dying,
Please don't let me go,
Even though you know.

Micky Whittle (13)
Newent Community School

Anger (PMT)

The little red devil creeps out
Screeches at the enemy
Eyes only see red. Eyes only see red
Firing nasty dialogue,
At war with the kitchen plates
Stabbing the loved ones in the heart
Straining their feelings, plucking their weak strings.
Gets the better of them, out of control.
She snaps and punches a fierce finishing line.
Suspense hangs over.
The burning madness cools off
Little angel's back, feeling guilty as *hell!*

Harriet Baynham-Williams (13)
Newent Community School

Moonlit Shadows

Steely-eyed hunter,
As still as a stone.
Stares into the darkness,
From high on his throne.

The cold bites deep,
Under the moon he lurks.
Ears pricked high,
He waits, alert.

Upon his gaze,
His prey does fall.
A feast enough,
To feed them all.

Snow stained scarlet,
They all attack.
But he remains,
The ace in the pack.

Luke Warren (14)
Newent Community School

Dying For A Drink

You look at me
Your eyes full of hate
And then I see
This is my fate
So why am I crying
As you're taken away
And I look on
The price I had to pay
For loving you as much as I did
So when we fought
You acted like a kid
But I guess you always were
When I think back through my tears
Remembering the times we played
We had no fears.
I call your name
But you cannot hear
Even if I yelled it in your ear
You see I'm writing this now
You are what I strive,
But I would still have you
If you didn't drink and drive.

Lucy Henderson (12)
Newent Community School

A Stormy Day

The rain is pouring
And the lightning is filling the sky.
Thunder is everywhere
Bang! Crash!
There goes the tree
Down to the ground outside.

Tap, tap, tap on the window
As the rain and hail hit.
Darkness has now fallen
And there's a smell of wet, damp clothes.

If the storm carries on,
the power is going to go out.
The trees are going to fall
Like the ones in the back garden.

The wind is violent
And the sound is hurting my ears,
Howling like a wolf.
The storm gets better
And the rain calms down,
The storm has passed,
It is over, no more storm.

Jo Daly (12)
Newent Community School

Snowy Day

When the wind is cold,
And the trees are bare,
The snow starts falling
Everywhere.
The children are happy,
The sleighs are out,
There's a magical feeling
All about!
It's slushy and cold,
Magical and white,
It's one of the most
Beautiful sights!
It's made from crystals
Of fun and joy,
It's like a child's
Brand new toy.
Snowmen are born
And snow angels too,
Footprints in the snow
Of a child's little shoe.
It's like a white blanket
Across the ground,
It floats down without
One single sound.

Rebecca Overbury (12)
Newent Community School

I Hear . . .

My school of sounds
That touches my ears
I listen . . .

Cars, buses, vehicles come.
Rustling, clanging, scraping on the road.
Scuffing from the children's shoes,
Stomp, they stop.
The bell.
Lessons to start with the talking and laughter.
Friends whispering, secrets trickle in my ears.
Bags emptied, clatter of pens.
Bang the door.
Teacher comes in with a thud.
Books slam down on her desk.
She barks and booms at the children, *'Quiet!'*
All listen. All see, all do.
Whispers creep up and scare like a ghost.
Talking gets louder then . . .
It stops.
Like water the silence flows around,
Pens scratching like an insect orchestra.
Scraping, stamping, crackling and creaking,
I look up into the clouds above,
All silent. All still.

Jess Huggins (12)
Newent Community School

Lonely Girl

Lonely girl, walk down the hall,
Pretend you don't hear them laughing,
You don't see them pointing,
Make yourself believe there's no one there.
Lonely girl, get on the bus,
Sit on your own and stare at your lap,
Pretend there's no one around.
Hold in your tears, don't let them see you cry,
Lonely girl, get off the bus,
Avoid the shouts and jeers,
Let them think you don't see the icy glares.
Walk home and still don't cry,
Don't let them see you cry.
Lonely girl, go to your room, close the door,
Close everyone out of your life.
If only you could do that.
Turn your music on loud, lie on your bed and cry.
Cry your worries and your problems away,
But don't worry they'll be back again tomorrow
And they'll be much worse.
But what can you do?
How much longer can you go on like this?
How much longer can you believe there's no one there?
How much longer can you stand to be a lonely girl?

Susanna Nolan (13)
Newent Community School

A Windy Day

A leaf rolls along the autumn path,
A whisper through the trees.
A smell of fresh, but rotting leaves,
Accompanies the air.
A flutter of one lost duck's wing,
The cry of a lonely crow.
The deserted path is full of leaves,
Crunching underfoot.
The splashing of a muddy pool,
And the darting of a squirrel.

The trees are now growing bare,
As leaves fall in a whirl of wind
And as this day rolls on,
Autumn's pumpkin-orange sky appears,
Just above the bitter air.
Leaves glowing with a frosty glaze,
Compost heaps are all full,
With plenty of leaves to spare.
A bitter wind has filled the air,
As a windy night draws in.

Conker shells are left behind,
As chestnuts go to war.
The distant crack of a hunter's gun,
Just ripples through the wind.
Now comes the honking of,
A migrating flock of geese.
The autumn, windy day tiers on,
The cold settles in,
The darkness now just fills the air,
The leaves are laid to rest.

Rupert Bailey (12)
Newent Community School

School's Out

School is out
There's no one about
The teachers have gone home
There's no one to moan
The classrooms are empty
There's no need to tempt me
Cos off I go
To pay back what I owe.

The air is so fine
It's clear and divine
There isn't a sound
No footstep on the ground
There's no more laughter
With detentions after
No more tears
Or showing your fears.

It's time to chill with all my mates
Where we will discuss our pet hates
Especially school
Cos it isn't cool
Apart from when the summer's here
Because it means it's the end of the year
Isn't it great? Isn't it fab?
No more time in the science lab.

Everything is in silence
There's no more violence
The term has finally come to an end
It's great cos now it's the weekend
Come and join us and have a laugh
Join in the fun of arts and craft.

Harrianne Burdett (12)
Newent Community School

I Love You Mum

Why me? Why her? Why now?
Just why?

I knew she was upset
I knew she'd cried every day since Dad left
Layers of clothes hid her body,
Self-destructive as mould.
I knew she thought I'd never realise,
I thought she loved me so why?

I thought she'd realise Dad was forever gone,
That I didn't want to lose her too.
I thought she knew she could get help,
I thought she knew I'd always be there for her.
I thought she knew I loved her,
But she'll never know how much.

I just see her there, hanging, purple face and hands.
She's never going to know,
Never going to hear me say and mean the words,
'I love you Mum.'

Rachel Hobby (13)
Newent Community School

Erik

My friend Erik is always there
He's there when I need comforting
He's there when I'm on a high
He's there when I'm lonely or with a frown.

Erik can change size whenever he wants
Small or large
Fat or thin
He sleeps on my pillow
Or under the stairs
My friend Erik is always there.

Even though my friends can't see him
He's always next to me
With a smile on his face
Never with a tear.

I love my friend Erik
He's my best friend (next to Glybalz)
We're like Batman and Robin
Friends till the end
My friend Erik.

Will Voss (13)
Newent Community School

A Stormy Day

The thunder and the howling winds,
The lightning and the rain.
The cyclone hits Jamaica
Striking harder and harder again.

Hailstones, the size of walnuts
Skim and skid along the ground.
The crackle of raging fire,
Ruins are all that are found.

A high-pitched scale on a piano
Is played by the mighty wind.
All the ground beneath it,
Is killed and then is skinned.

The sound is practically deafening,
The scene is a living hell.
Nothing is heard but the wind
Not even the old church bell.

Silence.
No noise.

The storm has left nothing
Unharmed.

Chris Dowle (12)
Newent Community School

The Cottage

Moonshine falls through the brooding trees,
Covering me with light.
I walk the overgrown forest path
Quietly afraid of the night.

The cottage looms ahead of me,
Abandoned, cold and dark.
The rotten door creaks open,
The silence as sharp as a dart.

I plunge into the building,
The damp air piercing my soul.
Fearing the worst I mount the stairs,
Dust covered, broken and old.

I see broken hearts, ruined lives,
The corpses and the blood.
I see the things this house has seen,
The scorch marks on the wood.

I leave the cottage burning,
Leave it to die, to be gone.
If anyone asks me what I have seen,
I'll say, 'Nothing, I saw no one.'

Harriet Evans (13)
Newent Community School

I Wish

I wish I had wings
So I could fly away,
I wish I had wings
To avoid another day.
I wish I had wings
And could leave this place,
I wish I had wings
So I don't have to see your face.
I wish I had wings
And spread them far,
I wish I had wings
So I could reach a shining star.
I wish I had wings
And could fly high in the sky,
I wish I had wings
So I couldn't hear one more lie.
And fly to an ocean blue,
I wish I had wings
Just if it meant I was away from you,
I wish I had wings
So I could fly away.

Jennifer Walker (13)
Newent Community School

Fog

Winter creeping up the path,
Frost knocks on the door,
Fog appears out of nowhere,
Creeping more and more.

Wisps of soulless wisps of smoke,
Touching, caressing skin,
Flowing, strangle, choke, choke, coke,
Letting night-time in.

A cloaked moon casting shadows,
The crackle of rain on roof,
Waiting in your warm home,
Hope your house is waterproof.

The screech of the owl swooping by,
Car lights blinding eyes,
Crunch of leaves, careful don't trip,
Fog is full of surprise.

The sun has won against the moon,
To shine the dark away,
The smell of dewdrop on the grass
And children come to play.

Emily Padley (12)
Newent Community School

Springtime

The end of Lent is nearly here,
People start to get into the Easter cheer,
As you hear the church bells ring,
It sounds like listening to the song birds sing.

The flowers are blooming here and there,
The daffodils are everywhere,
Their trumpets glistening in the lengthening sunlight,
Bulbs pushing through the ground with all their might.

The trees are gaining their colourful leaves,
That were stolen by the autumn wind thieves.
Bright is a springtime colour,
Green as can be and given by nature's mother.

The new start is all around,
Animals give birth on the colourful ground.
Springtime is such a happy time of year,
More light, new colour, new life is here.

Jesus did a long time ago,
We still praise him as we know,
He died on the cross but came back to life,
Remember this at Easter.

Gemma Prince (12)
Newent Community School

A Smile

A smile.
It starts with a smile,
Coy, powerful, beautiful,
It frees your heart,
Takes you places you've never been before,
When from the one you love.

A smile.
A sign to bring it further,
It bridges the gap,
Controls your relationship,
Changes your life,
When from the one you love.

A smile.
It never comes,
Disappointing, bitter,
You want to see it,
You never do,
Never from the one you love.

I will always be waiting,
Waiting for a smile.

Thomas Farr (15)
Newent Community School

Emus

One day I saw an emu
Living on a farm.
It wasn't very active,
As it was sleeping in a barn.

With lots of sounds and noises
Coming from a shed,
I took a look inside it
And saw an emu in a bed!

I drove back home in my car,
And I saw another emu,
This time,
Drinking in a bar!

I wasn't very happy,
When I got home that night,
As I saw yet another emu,
And it was playing with my kite!

Matthew Ward (12)
Newent Community School

Autumn

Autumn all around us,
It's in the air everywhere,
It's crisp and clear,
As winter draws near.

Cheryl Cooper (13)
Newent Community School

My Quad Bike

With its big, chunky tyres,
100cc engine,
And red metallic paintwork,
My quad looks the best around.

I slam the kick-start down,
Let the engine warm up,
Then I'm ready, and off!

I'm flying round,
Nothing gets in my way.
My mind, my thoughts,
Get pushed away.
I focus on the finishing line.

I'm neck and neck with number nine,
I pass him on the last corner,
With a massive smile upon my face.

Hannorah Stephens (14)
Newent Community School

A Snowy Day

Snowy days are so exciting
The glittering snow softly falling
It's cold, but has a warm feeling
A sheet of white with children screaming
The red children's noses glowing bright
Waiting for a visitor to come in the night.
Crunch on the ice can't wait to go sledging.
Don't be late you'll miss turkey and pudding
When you get a breath of fresh air
Then all your problems go somewhere
Finally the snow starts to go
And another cold wind starts to blow.

Sarah Phillips (12)
Newent Community School

Jim-Bobby Jim-Moore!

Right deep down on the ocean floor,
There was a little, old cottage with a little, old door.
It was home to a fish called Jim-Bobby Jim-Moore,
He was colourful and special and really, really small.

He swiftly swam through the open sea,
Through all the seaweed,
He was filled with glee.
With his colourful fins and his shiny tail,
On his travels he came across a big, fat whale.

The whale was big,
Not like the fish,
When he swam the tide went in.
He was black and white and big and tall,
But the little old fish was really small.

So on he swam, alone once more.
The little old fish Jim-Bobby Jim-Moore.

Charmaine Evans (12)
Newent Community School

Foggy Days

Foggy days aren't the best,
It's hard to see for miles,
With lots of energy you don't rest,
You want to play on those piles.

It's quiet with an eerie silence,
The crackle of a leafy mess,
Shows the vague images in the distance,
It will come closer if it's careless.

The cloud overrules the sky,
Just wait the sun will show,
When you see a bird fly,
You know the sun will glow.

Nicola Thurston (12)
Newent Community School

A Jump Too Far

So sorry Mum, so sorry Dad,
I knew I sometimes drove you mad.
I didn't mean to cause you pain,
I knew I was a bit insane.

I'm sorry for the drugs and smoking,
You all thought that I was joking.
Now that Jake and I are over,
I feel oh so sad and sober.

Kate and Carrie left me there,
I really thought that they did care.
My life was really close to Hell,
Even though you could not tell.

I felt let down and so afraid,
Surely now I must have paid
For all the harm that I did cause,
Millie, now I'm always yours.

Alice Murphy (13)
Newent Community School

Literary Dreams

My dreams are of musicals and plays,
Of Shakespeare's sonnets and lazy days,
Of love, food and drink,
Of lightning, thunder and ships that sink,
As murder strikes in the evening air,
My peaceful dream fills me with despair,
As plots and schemes drift round my head,
I curl up tightly in my bed,
A witch's cackle echoes through the room,
I sit bolt upright staring at the moon,
I slide beneath my covers shivering with fear,
Praying that dawn will soon be near,
A hooting owl is the last I hear.

Kate Richards (13)
Newent Community School

A Snowy Day

The air is as cold as ice
and as the snow glitters, nice.
Log fires are burning in people's homes,
trying to warm up their red shiny nose.
You hear crunches beneath your feet,
because it's still and quiet out on the street.
In the morning as you awake,
you see a single white snowflake.
Children play snowball fights,
underneath the bright street lights.
The cold wind sweeps off the floor
and then makes its way through
the gaps in your door.
Because the soft snow fell all night,
it left behind its sheet of white.

Tanya Oliver-Burns (12)
Newent Community School

A Snowy Day

I look outside
I see a white carpet of snow
How fun
I run outside
Crunch, squelch, crunch
It's cold outside
I see a robin singing
His beautiful song
It's getting colder
The white carpet of snow
Is covered in footprints
I've ruined the white
Carpet of snow
I go in.

Chloe Hopper (12)
Newent Community School

My Little Green Faeries

The faeries were playing amongst the grass of light
Their wings were full and ready to take flight
They sat, they flew, they jumped and rolled
Then whooshed back home to their magical tree of mould.

The tree was tall, strong and bright
The faeries had protected it with all their might
For centuries they guarded, secured and latched
Just waiting for the goblins who longed to snatch.

A labyrinth of imps, sprites, mermaids, trolls
Fortified these lands like little rag dolls
Seen as slaves, keepers and custodian alike
These imprisoned 'rag dolls' rebelled with might.

The labyrinth had turned its back. Shut its doors
The magical tree was no more
My little green faeries still fly the night skies,
Searching for their lost, their stolen; their magical tree had died.

Stacey Evans (16)
Newent Community School

Who Am I?

Are you one of those people who like to stay in bed
Or are you one of those people who find excitement in a shed?
Do you always ask questions, who, what, how and where
Or do you do boring and sit at home and stare?
Are you a sporty one who's always down the park
Or are you one of those junkies that get drunk after dark?

I know what I am
Do you know who you are?
You should!

Matt Siddle (13)
Newent Community School

The Polar Bear

The polar bear, the polar bear,
He has a handsome coat to wear.

His coat is thick, warm and white.
He wears it throughout the night.

He likes to have a lot to eat.
His favourite meal is made of meat.

He lives with his mum and dad
And he thinks his dad is mad!

He likes to play around all day.
Normally in the month of May.

He cuddles up with his fox.
He wishes he had socks.

I love to watch the polar bears
And I love the white coat they wear.

Amelia Cornish (12)
Newent Community School

The Well-Loved Panda

Black and white,
Hidden in the night.
Eating bamboo,
Has a friend called Roo.

He is a panda who is shy,
And there in the forest he does lie.
Waiting for his prey to come,
Silent as ever, ready to run.

Very quiet while he sleeps,
Here comes a car, bleep, bleep, bleep.
He has been captured and taken away,
The animals wonder if he will be OK.

Samantha Brockbank (12)
Newent Community School

Panda Poem

Black and white
Hidden in the night
Eating bamboo
Has a friend called Roo.

Very quiet while he sleeps
Suddenly a noise, which bleep, bleep, bleeps.
He has been captured and taken away
The animals wondered if he'd be OK.

He came back the very next morning
When his friends greeted him whilst he was yawning,
'Where have you been?' they all cried
'To the moon and back,' he lied.

He got to his feet and turned away
Walked off with his friends and went to play!

Francesca Moss (12)
Newent Community School

My Hope

The orange ball of fire has gone
I run, where has it gone?
Please come back you are my only hope
The darkness settles around me like a thick blanket
But I don't want it!
I want the sun,
I want the day,
I want the freedom,
I want to live.
I don't want to fall into the dark,
I want to run,
But the sun has gone, my time is up.
The darkness swallows me up,
There is no place for me anymore,
My time is up.

Jess Butler (13)
Newent Community School

What's Happened To My Grandad?

How must it feel to not understand?
You need someone beside you, holding your hand,
A life with no stability, a life with no pride,
What happens when there's nobody there by your side?

As long as you have family, as long as you have friends,
You have help beside you, that they're willing to lend,
They love you so dearly; they love you so much,
So sad most things around you must seem like double Dutch.

It's so good to see you smiling; it so good to see you laugh,
Having a good sing song, songs from the past,
Going out to your centre, meeting people new,
Your eyes are sparkling again, like little drops of dew.

Dementia is this illness; it makes you so confused,
How hard it is for you to give your different points of view,
You can't remember people's names, but that won't bother us,
Because we know, deep down in you, you love us very much!

Emily Page (11)
Ribston Hall High School

Fireworks

They rise like sudden growing flowers
that fly upon the night
Then fall to Earth in burning streams
of crimson, blue and white.
Like buds too wonderful to name,
each miracle unfolds
And Catherine wheels begin to flame
like whirling marigolds.
Rockets and Roman candles
make an orchard of the sky,
Whence magic trees' leaves
shake upon each gazing eye.

Emilie Levett (11)
Ribston Hall High School

Getting To School

I yawn and stretch I'm wide awake,
I'd better get up or I will be late,
In the bathroom, I must go,
'Hurry up,' Mum is shouting,
'You're too slow.'

Back in my bedroom,
Adjusting my tie,
I'm looking quite good,
I must not lie.

I'm eating my breakfast really quite fast,
While Mum is busy filling flasks,
Now it is nearly time to go,
I must put on my coat,
Strap on my bag,
Out the door we go.

At the school we arrive,
Watching the playground come alive,
The bell rings, time to go,
So 'Bye Mum, cheerio!'

Laura Phillips (12)
Ribston Hall High School

I Like . . .

In winter I like a warm bed,
But the cold side of a pillow.
I like the smell of our roast turkey.

I love the way my dad dresses the tree,
I love the way my presents are wrapped,
I love playing with my new toys.

I like the way my face glows
After I have been in the snow,
I like to see the snow angels and footprints.
These are my memories.

Lauren Moore (12)
Ribston Hall High School

When I Grow Old

Once,
I heard my granny say,
'When I am gone remember me.

Treasure my memories,
To help with your difficult times,
For they are the healers of life
And may bring happiness to your world.

I've had good times and bad,
A day of love as warm as the sun's rays.
Drops of my heart making new paths,
Dust settling over destroyed lives and the loved.'

She stopped and stared.
There and then she said;
'Take time to enjoy life while you have the chance.'

Ellie Hetenyi (12)
Ribston Hall High School

Why War?

Why do we have war?
What is the point of the killing?

War has no meaning,
Just pointless life loss,
Who wants to waste precious life?
Only cruel, heartless people,
Who have nothing better to do.

Feel sorry for the people,
Whose lives have been torn in two,
For no apparent reason,
Only because of colour or race,
If you were one of these people,
Would you sit and weep,
Or would you speak up to those who are wrong?

Rebecca Davies (11)
Ribston Hall High School

Religious Studies

R eligious studies is so cool,
E very lesson will teach you something new,
L ord our God will teach the rule,
I f you learn something, others could too!
G ot to be kind, never be rude,
I n different cultures, people may live in a different way,
O n top of all that, you can try new food!
U pstairs some people may choose to pray,
S ometimes people have religious names.

S ome people believe in different things,
T o some of us religion can seem stranger,
U nusual hymns that people do sing,
D iscover new festivals and keeping from danger,
I f ever you're stuck or don't understand,
E ven if you feel you are on your own -
S imply ask God to lend a hand!

Sasha Palmer (11)
Ribston Hall High School

The Apple Pie

There it lays on the table
with its golden coat.
I wondered what would lie within.
I picked it up,
trying not to spoil its beauty.
I opened my mouth slowly
then closed it again.
I was silent for a moment
taking in the juice.
Then I decided
this was the best apple pie.
I took another bite straight away.

Louise Nichols (11)
Ribston Hall High School

Listen And Hear

Shhhhh!
Sit very, very still
And listen.

Listen to waves,
Crashing against rock
In the ocean blue.

Listen to sand,
Dropping from buckets
Crashing against the floor.

Listen to wind,
Blowing the sand
Across the beach.

Listen to fire,
Blazing deeply
On Guy Fawkes.

Listen to trees,
Blowing in the wind
High above the ground.

Listen to all these sounds,
Sit very, very still
Listen and hear.

Sheri-Ann Chaloner (11)
Ribston Hall High School

I Wonder What Will Happen In The Future

I wonder what will happen in the future,
I wonder how will they travel.
Will they travel by car or bus?
Will they travel at all?

I wonder what they will look like,
Will they look like you and me?
I wonder how old they will live to,
Older than you and me?

I wonder if they'll go to school,
I wonder if they will still get homework.
I wonder what they'll do for fun,
Would they still have fun?

I wonder if they'll still have computers,
I wonder if they'll still have TV.
I wonder if they'd still go shopping,
Or if they'd just stay at home and watch TV.

I wonder if they'll go on holiday,
Or to the beach.
I wonder if they could still swim
And will they still have the Olympics.

I suppose all I can do is wonder!

Cassie Hann (12)
Ribston Hall High School

An Old English Poem

Thy watch the child out in the snow,
As thy drink from thy goblet,
Lonely, upset, her wondrous soul,
Travels night to dawn to find,
The key that fits the lock and combines,
To create the happiness and joyful life,
This is all her 'eart and soul desires,
A family, a loving caring family,
But where she will find this wish of her dreams,
Is beyond knowledge,
As this town has cold-hearted people.

Christmas is drawing near,
St Nicholas is soon going to be here,
The child's eyes drop a tear each,
That trickles down her pale face to the ground,
And freezes, her legs give way and she fell to the snowy floor,
Her eyes are now a river of continuous tears,
Streaming down her face,
She looks up to the sky but instead sees St Nicholas,
Gazing down at her, in a crumpled heap in front of him.

'Child I heard your wish, I'll grant it as all should enjoy Christmas.'

Jordan Gardiner (11)
Ribston Hall High School

Grandpa

Grandpa, he really does enjoy the summer,
He sits in his chair, rocking away singing with the birds,
He needs help really; his mind and body are shutting down,
Although he'll never admit it.

He'll sit in the basement, tired and speechless,
Just sitting on the steps,
Looking at all the pictures of late grandma,
He knows she's gone and he soon will be too.

The desperation in his eyes,
You can tell he's in agony,
But he won't admit it to anyone,
In case they think he's weak and needs help.

He's always so stubborn,
He won't even let Poppa help him on his way,
He likes things done his way and no one else's,
And we don't complain in case he gets restless.

Grandpa, he really enjoys the winter,
To curl up under his rug,
And fall into deep sleep,
He would prefer to go that way.

Vanessa Smith (12)
Ribston Hall High School

Friendship

Little drops of water,
Little grains of sand,
Make the mighty ocean,
And the colourful land!

All the little moments,
Horrible they may see,
Make a difference,
Of how our friendship is meant to be!

So our little errors and mistakes,
Will drift away,
And make our friendship,
Stronger each and every day!

Little deeds of kindness,
Little deeds of friendship from you and me,
Will make our bond,
As strong as it can be!

So like the drops of water,
And the grains of sand,
We will combine together,
To make the ocean and the land!

Amy Wright-Hamilton (12)
Ribston Hall High School

Whatever She Is

I know a girl called Patsy-Sue
She lives in a village in Timbuktu.

She sends me cards every day
So I reply, 'I'm busy - OK!'

She once even threw a disco for tea
That Patsy-Sue embarrassed me.

I know her from my primary school
She was clumsy, a great big fool.

Her teeth are crooked, her fingernails yuck
And her soggy thumb she used to suck!

She called me Kate, oh I hate that name
And she knows that it brings me shame.

So one day she knocked on my door
I opened it and . . . fell to the floor.

'Why, why, why are you here today?'
'I've brought you a plate made of clay!'

'I'll keep it safe, thanks a lot Sue
Now I've gotta go, I need the loo.'

'Well that's a shame, I've come all this way.'
'Well sorry Sue, come another day.'

She's wild and quirky with hair that's frizz
But she's still my friend, *whatever she is.*

Katie McWhannell (11)
Ribston Hall High School

Crying

Looking out of the window,
Watching the world go by,
The raindrops trickling down,
Like the tears in my eye.
The clouds making shapes,
All fluffy and white,
Everything seems to have gone wrong,
Through the days and the nights.
My whole world's been turned upside down,
All because of one little girl,
The fight caused me to regret something big,
Everything was in a whirl.
I lashed out first,
Then she pushed me to the floor,
I was sent to see Miss,
She gave me a lecture about law.
She pressured me to do it,
She laughed and called me names,
Then everybody joined in,
And it was no longer a game.
Miss told me I was bad,
I tried to explain it wasn't me,
But she would not listen,
She told me I was to leave.
As I walked down the hall,
Everything went quiet,
Here I am now crying and crying.

Alex McLaughlin (12)
Ribston Hall High School

Silence

A scream
A scream

Silence.

Finally it's finished, we walk away;
Smiling and laughing.
Praising each other because of our achievements.

Singing our favourite song, we hum along;
Skipping and running,
Shouting over disagreements.

Then we make up, like pen to paper;
Hugging, cross the road which awaits us.

Ran out without looking,
Though I told her to stop.
Crying, hearing the squeal of brakes.

From the loudest sound I've ever heard,
A scream
A scream . . .

To silence!

Rebecca Wasley (12)
Ribston Hall High School

Motorway

Driving along the deadly motorway,
Are motorbikes, lorries, vans and cars,
Smoke and fumes pollute the sky,
As grey clouds pass over and by.
Beeping horns, 'Get out the way,'
Road hogs take control,
Chris Moyles on Radio One,
Keeping the whole family amused,
The sweet scent of air freshener,
Brightens up your day.

Daniel O'Driscoll (14)
The Cotswold School

Tropical Paradise

In the middle of the Caribbean,
An island was found,
It had a jungle,
And its shape was round.

The sun shone down,
On the crystal-blue sea,
A monkey could be heard,
From up in a tree.

The smell of the fruits,
Wafting in the air,
On this island,
You'd be without a care.

It's so tranquil,
With no pollution at all,
The best tropical paradise,
Even though it's quite small.

Chris Miles (13)
The Cotswold School

Fast Food Shop

B urgers are burnt in a fast food shop,
E qually are chips to make them top,
E ager are employees to satisfy customers,
F rying themselves in big fat jumpers,
Y ou'd better be pleased or they'd get the chop.

B eefy worker runs to get a mop,
U nfortunately a child just puked over the floor,
R efusing is Mum, to stay as she walks out the door,
G reedy customers eating the place out of stock,
E mployee looking at the clock waiting for his break, tick-tock,
R eady is the place to close as they leave ready for bed,
S till is a cleaner cleaning, cleaning till his hands are red.

Daniel Binding (13)
The Cotswold School

Chocolate

Tall, dark and handsome,
Is what chocolate means to me,
It's something I can never resist,
It makes me feel happy!

Plain, milk, marble and white,
Are all my favourite flavours,
Truffles, fudges, nuts and flakes,
Can spark off bad behaviour!

Romantically, it's a great success,
And wins over many hearts,
Emotionally, it can bring you down,
Depression, it's worst part.

The sweetness of the taste,
Makes temptation seem so easy,
The richness of the aroma,
OK, now I feel quite queasy.

Amy Hubbard (13)
The Cotswold School

Tropical Paradise

Calm surroundings, the smell of fresh air,
Sand on your feet, salt in your hair.

Laughing and splashing, a few palm trees,
Snorkellers gazing at the artistic coral reef.

Steel drums, shells and tropical fish,
A plate of fresh fruit,
What a succulent dish.

Running through the white, luscious sand,
Dying to hold that crystal clear water in my hand.

Sun is gleaming, slap the sunblock on,
Make the most of this paradise because
We're soon to be gone!

Amy Denny (13)
The Cotswold School

Paradise

The white sand between my toes and the shining sun
                                        burning down,
This paradise makes me happy, do anything but frown,
Around me, the sounds of trees swaying and the sea
                                        kissing the sand,
Walking up the beach, touching sparkling water with my hand,
The smell of fresh grown fruit is wafting up into my nose,
All around me is tropical flowers, a change from the English rose,
Excitement builds inside me, so lucky to be here,
The sea is calling out to me and as I'm getting near,
My legs can't help but run to this salt-smelling sea,
Down with the tropical fish I long to be,
Starting to get hot now, so find shade under a palm,
Climb up to get a coconut, can't come to any harm.
Crack it open on a rock, the succulent milk drips on my lips,
I get a rush of happiness, from my toes to my fingertips,
But now it's time to leave, say goodbye to this amazing place,
And as I leave the sand, the smile also leaves my face.

Jasmine Burns (13)
The Cotswold School

On The M1

Honking horns, angry voices,
These are all traffic jam noises,
Rising gas, fumes and dust,
Peeling paint and flaking rust,
Crackling radios and corny old tapes,
Thundering lorries with England drapes,
Motorcycles race away,
Like hungry animals chasing prey,
But while this is all going on,
A cloud of smog blocks out the sun.

Alexander Jess (13)
The Cotswold School

Tropical Paradise

You are away in a tropical paradise,
Laying on the yellow sand of the beach,
With the wind blowing through your hair,
Sea, miles of sea and sand around you.

The smell of sea salt rushes up your nose,
You wish you could stay in this dream land forever,
But you know you have to leave tomorrow,
You will leave the luscious tropical fruit behind,
The coconuts, bananas will all be gone.

The night comes around fast,
You lay in your five-star suite,
Thinking you cannot go home,
The last flight home is here,
You will never forget this holiday . . .
Until the next year.

Jason Eakins (13)
The Cotswold School

Takeaways

You ring them up and they deliver,
Chips, cod and also liver,
There's lots of different takeaways,
Some do fish, but not always.

You can pick it up in your car,
As normally they're never far,
Or they'll bring it to your door,
Then you won't miss your team score.

Throw the diet out the door,
But you're not hungry anymore,
No washing up needs to be done,
Just sit back and have some fun.

Max Lewis Yates (14)
The Cotswold School

Traffic Jam

Today there was a traffic jam,
All because of a crash,
Ranting and raving motorists,
Beeping their horns with a bash.

Shrieking club music booming,
Piercing everyone's ears,
Novice drivers apprehensive,
The clueless boys are drinking beers.

Foul fumes inflate the air,
As all the engines rev,
A man's car has broken down
It doesn't seem to rev.

Soon I know I will be home,
As the cars start to clear,
We move along at a speed,
Fumes dwindle and disappear.

Louise Finch (13)
The Cotswold School

Magic

Ghosts, owls and monsters,
All creatures of the night,
Magic forces stirring,
The candles glowing bright.

The dead become alive,
What is this magic spell?
Magic forces stirring,
The Earth, becoming hell.

As this voodoo cowers,
The creatures of the night,
Return to where they came from,
And darkness returns to light.

Emily Seal (13)
The Cotswold School

Moments In Paradise!

Waves lapping, reaching the shore,
Trees swaying in the gentle breeze,
The sound of planes, airborne overhead,
A bikini babe and a tanned boy with a six-pack,
Heat haze in the distance, tan on your back.

Beach towels, like patchwork lay on the beach,
Heat protection, your bodies covered in cream,
Sizzling red-raw faces, exposed to the sun,
Young kids in T-shirts, leaping in the sea,
Lazing on the water's flow, on a blown-up lilo.

The prolonged journey,
Back home to true life's here,
Not realising the end was so near,
Coming back, gliding through the sky,
Britain's approaching, half the world's gone by!

Kelly Long (14)
The Cotswold School

Beach

B eyond the horizon far, far, away,
E erie little predators come out to pray,
A ll the little fish swim far away,
C ome to the beaches where we're all having fun,
H ide in the coral under the golden sun.

I n the dead of night the boat roared away,
N ever to return until the next day.

T he waves are twirling, the waves are booming,
H ere is where all the fish are looming,
E mbedded here under the sand, all shells lie ready to be found.

S o one day when the weather's calm,
U nder the sand lie fish unknown,
N ever to be disturbed again.

James Granger (13)
The Cotswold School

Demon's Tears

The man rose his blade high,
While the demon circled around him about to die,
With the shield of faith guarding his life,
He was about to end the torment and strife,
Stepping forward he delivered the blow,
The blade bit deep and low,
The demon shrieked with pain and awe,
This man's strength was true it saw,
Staggering around with a gash in its thigh,
The blasphemous demon began to cry,
With tears of molten fire it started to drop,
But the man gave no pity and began to chop,
His moment was true and his timing was right,
The demon gave him no last fight.

Finally the valiant hero came to rest,
Knowing that he had done his best.

Oliver Sketchley-Kaye (13)
The Cotswold School

A Hectic Day

It's a very hectic day,
People determined to get first in the queue,
Hungry children run to their parents,
Dirty tables smouldered in ketchup and chips,
Squashed into the dirty floor.

Sizzling burgers on a hot grill,
Customers come and go, there is money in the till,
Drinks being splashed and ice cubes being shattered,
Busy workers have no time,
The restaurant soon closes at half-past nine,
As the manger locks the door, she peeks
Through the window making sure everything is fine.

Hannah May Williams (14)
The Cotswold School

Sun, Sand And Sea

Sand shuffling between my toes,
Wind through my hair,
People bathing in the sea,
And the smell of plain fresh air.

The waves lapping onto the beach,
The ice cream man is here,
Girls lying on the sand,
And men with a pint of beer.

The women trying to get a tan,
By relaxing in the sun,
This spot is really great,
And you can have some fun.

Racing through the waves,
Plunging into the sea,
I want to stay here forever,
My family and me.

Tom Jess (13)
The Cotswold School

Perfect Paradise

Blue glistening waves lapping on the shore,
The sun beating down more and more,
The sound of strange, orange birds,
The wild boar coming to the shore, in herds,
A tiny little boat, like a pea out at sea,
And the sound of a buzzing bee,
One lonely cloud up in the sky,
As monkeys swinging from trees, seem to fly,
The soft sparkly sand goes on for miles,
And the temperature can't be measured by dials,
A wooden hut at the end of the beach,
There in a distant sound of holidaymakers, with an ice cream each,
As a gentle breeze like a hand,
Sweeping gracefully over the land,
You're the only one to be found,
Beneath your feet you can hardly feel the ground,
Stop!
Look around,
And take in this perfect paradise.

Samantha Norman (14)
The Cotswold School

Love On The M25

With a heavy heart, he joins the queue,
And remembers how badly he needs the loo,
He glumly glares out to his left,
And watches a bird soar into its nest.
'How strange is it?' he began to ponder,
'That beauty can be found wherever you wander.'
He sat back uncomfortably in his seat,
And listened to the radio's droning beat,
In the ignition the keys did jangle,
As the traffic creeps on in their tailing tangle,
The man blankly stares out to his right,
And his eyes behold a bewitching sight.
A woman seated in the car next to him,
With sweet pink lips and golden brown skin.
'She's the most beautiful creature I ever did see,
Could there be a chance, she could fall for me?'
She turned to him through the windowpane,
And smiled with the knowledge that she felt the same.
On through the traffic they both did drive,
After love was formed on the M25.

Katharine Clissold (14)
The Cotswold School

Kids In The Car!

They play *I spy* again and again,
These kids are driving me round the bend,
How many crisps can one child eat?
Oh why do children have smelly feet?
Their shoes are circulating round the car,
They've hit twice, they're pushing me far,
I try so hard to keep my cool,
But then the chimps start to drool,
I tell the small one to blow his nose,
And remove his mouth from his toes,
How long can I put up with this?
I was made for pampering, love and bliss.
At last I see a light turn green,
We start to move, the children scream,
At least they're happy, feeling good,
They haven't yet reached adulthood,
Although this car drive seemed like hell,
It rung a familiar childhood bell,
I used to be like those chimpanzees,
Silly and crazy, young and free,
So why shouldn't I sing with glee?
Those monkey babes, are just like me!

Jessica Broadbent (13)
The Cotswold School

Supposed Paradise

No kids running, babies yelling,
Used nappies really smelling,
The clearest sea you ever saw,
You won't want anything anymore.
Everything's pure, nothing stinks,
White beaches and funky drinks,
A quiet night in, or a loud one out,
Fun is what it's all about.
The sea is like a remedy, a magic potion,
Trips around the island diving in the ocean.
The sun shining every day,
Washing all your worries away,
But when the time comes and the tide is rising,
Storms are coming, get into hiding!
Tropical hurricanes, tearing through,
There's nothing anyone can do,
The waves are booming,
Young couples, no longer swooning,
A widow wondering, will she join her husband at last?
The wind is rising, in short sharp blasts,
People crying, wanting dry land,
The thing you pray won't happen on a tropical island.

Catherine Chilton (13)
The Cotswold School

Desert Island

Marooned on a desert island,
A lone pirate confined,
No one left to talk to,
And all because of crimes.

Fantasising of a better place,
Where everybody knows his name,
A lone pirate dreams,
Of fair and worthy fame.

But living on the island,
Isn't really that dire,
He made himself a shelter,
And lit a giant fire.

Lots of fruit and coconuts,
To keep him fit and strong,
Yet still he itched for home,
But the journey was too long.

Lies, betrayal and devious plots,
Was why he was marooned,
He'd shot a load of people,
And blew up buildings too!

Would there ever be a boat
Sailing on the horizon?
No, nobody ever came,
No boats, no ships, no one.

Sarah Brown (13)
The Cotswold School

Seaside Mayhem

The sea is calm,
But not for long,
The kids are about,
It's time for fun,
Parents getting the sunblock out,
But kids ignoring them and running about.

The sea is now packed,
The day has now started,
No time to be bored,
The dinghies are out and on the water,
Adults are sunbathing,
Kids screaming, 'More, more!'

It's now creeping up to lunchtime,
The sea's getting calmer,
Screaming kids saying, 'No, no, no,'
The beach is virtually empty,
But cafés and restaurants packed
But soon all will be on the beach.

The beach is getting packed again,
Kids are piling into the water,
Parents screaming wait,
Dads acting like children,
Off to have some fun.

But the day is getting darker,
Families packing away and leaving,
The beach is looking calmer than ever,
Until tomorrow morning.

Lucy Boote (13)
The Cotswold School

My Paradise Island

Waves gently lapping on the sand,
The rough touch of the coconut that
I hold in my hand.

Above me an infinite expanse of blue sky,
With small fluffy clouds sailing by.

The buzzing of insects in a tall palm tree,
The serene pale green of a tropical sea.

The sand warm and golden between my toes,
The scent of sea salt as it blows past my nose.

Exotic flowers and sun-kissed fruits,
The gentle singing of birds as sweet as flutes.

The trees calmly swaying in a cooling breeze,
The sun slowly tanning my legs and my knees.

On my paradise island, far, far away,
Is where I forever long to stay.

Sarah Hulbert (13)
The Cotswold School

The Snake!

I can slither across the grass and hide from my teacher
and not go to school.
I can eat my sister, I am eating her straight away.
I can live in land and water, I wonder if I could fly?
I can be all different colours and at the moment I am black
with pink and black spots.
I can be thin or fat, long or short which depends on what species I am.
I can be cobra, anaconda or even a viper.
I can be deadly.
I can be harmless (a slow-worm or a grass snake - depending
on how you treat them.)
Some of my friends can even climb into trees and jump out.

Sam Mincher (11)
Thomas Keble School

The Crocodile

I am the angriest of them all,
The creatures great and small,
I snap at anything near,
Faster than running deer,
My scales glisten in the sun,
I'm always up for a bit of fun,
I swim faster than a fish,
Which also makes a tasty dish,
I have a beautiful tail,
Which is sharper than a nail,
I live in a river,
Be careful, I may eat your liver,
I lay eggs in the ground,
Which makes me very proud,
My wonderful long claws,
Are silkier than drawers,
I hunt for my food,
If I don't get any,
I get in a bad mood,
I am a meat eater,
Better than a cheetah.

Kristina Peart (11)
Thomas Keble School

The Hawk

He grabs tightly to the fish with stiffened talons,
Near the sea and open water,
Upright with pride, enclosed by the azure world he perches.

The deafening sea of terror beneath him roars defiantly,
He stares morosely from his mountain position,
And like a lightning bolt he descends.

Tom Heavisides (16)
Thomas Keble School

The Bunny Rabbit

I can be tame, I can be bold, but I'm really rather shy,
I'm smaller than a dog or cat, though I'm bigger than a fly.
I'm not that vicious and compared to a lion I don't really bite,
I am all so very colourful, I can be brown, black or white.
I'm so clever cos I can run, dig, jump or hop,
I'm sometimes found in a field, sometimes in a shop.
I really love carrots, I love to chew and munch,
I'd watch out for that sly old fox or he'll eat me for his lunch.
That farmer's always chasing me saying, 'Rabbit stew',
He doesn't have to be so mean, I have feelings too.
I've been told one hundred times I'm so very soft,
That's why they take care of me when I slightly cough.
I like to eat lots and lots, I'm really not that fussed,
They buy me a lot of new toys when my old ones bust.
Every night I go to sleep, I go to my hutch,
I really know my owners love me very, very much.
My cousin, the hare, has ears so tall,
Where mine are floppy and they just wobble down and fall.
They like to call me 'Bunny', it's their little habit,
But that's a lie cos I'm a little bunny rabbit.

Annie Chaplin (11)
Thomas Keble School

Spiders

If I were a spider I'd be a big one like a tarantula,
So I could live in a jungle and eat flies and bugs.
I'd also hide in trees then jump out when I saw a creature.
I'd be a brownie colour so I could blend in with the trees
And be camouflaged.
I would have 20 children and teach them to hunt like a lion.
I would also be able to swim when the jungle flooded.

Jack Reeves (11)
Thomas Keble School

Worm's Eye View

The drumming of rain is in my ears,
Cascading and rolling as I sit.
Time suspended,
A blackout from that evil thing called life.
Oh how I hate it,
And how it hates me.

I am the dreg of society,
What is my purpose?
I work hard for near nothing,
And I sit here in my trailer.
Trailer trash is no life,
But it is mine.

So I'll watch my TV set,
See how other people live.
Rich people, who know what living is,
I see it all from my worm's eye view.

Matt Howson (15)
Thomas Keble School

If I Was A Millionaire

If I was a millionaire,
I'd get a professional to do my hair,
I'd buy lots of diamond rings,
And I'd buy some clothes and things!

If I was a millionaire,
I'd become a massive star,
And then with all my money,
I'd buy a really flash car,
And then when I'm really rich,
I might buy a football pitch!

Amelia Davis (11)
Thomas Keble School

Jumping The Waves

I am a water baby
I love the sea

Whatever the weather
The ocean is the place to be

I love to jump the waves
Like the hurdles on a race track

I remember being a young child
And the excitement bubbling up

The waves seem to gallop towards us so quickly
To my dad's gigantic hands, I held on so tight

The fresh smell of sweet sea air
Seems to set the mind free

I would love to play at the seaside all day
I would never have any cares.

Jessamine Valentine (15)
Thomas Keble School

Lake Fairies

Water curled about her
Like crystal streams of pale moonlight
Which charms the air
There she stood by forest side
With all of fairies' grace
Deep in the woods and along the rocky shores
Over the still lake
Cold wind like ocean breeze
Ripple the water that surrounds her toes
And with a surge of pearl-white
She dives into the cool
Into the water in which she dwells.

Ruth Seager (15)
Thomas Keble School

My Pride And Joy

I'm her creation
Her own masterpiece
I love her more than the world's contents
I look up to her like I look up to the sky
High, high and higher

My memories of good days out
Hot, sunny days
I only have photographs to remind me
Our time together is precious
It doesn't last long

Dark, gloomy days
Anger and hatred
Is thrown across the room
The atmosphere speaks for itself

A limited hug and my presence
Is all that's there
We are close but so
Far away.

Alishia Newman (15)
Thomas Keble School

1989

An important year for all,
As life begins within a room,
The look on the face of the small infant,
The button nose and tiny toes,
The small, strong hands,
Squeezes with all its might,
In 1989 life had finally begun,
Smiles all round with tears too,
Two proud parents full with relief,
As the tiny infant screams,
Life began in 1989.

Kellyanne Vickers (15)
Thomas Keble School

My Best Friend And Me

My best friend and me
Have been together since we were three
We've helped each other when we were sad
We've both turned our lives around

We've made each other snort
When we thought we were naught
I've made her mad
When I was constantly sad

We look the same
But who's to blame?
We find the same jokes funny
We're always after our dad's for money

We've always had the same fears
For all of the past 12 years
We've been on trips
And had our blips

When she goes away I miss her loads
I'm always jealous of her clothes
But one thing is for sure
I couldn't ask for much more.

Sophie Whitfield (15)
Thomas Keble School

I Know This Girl . . .

I know this girl, she's as beautiful as could be,
Her bleach blonde hair and the black underneath,
Her eyes so gorgeous, they glow like the moon,
And a face so pretty, it's like roses in bloom.
Her personality is as soft as a kitten,
But when she gets mad you know you've been bitten,
But what I just said please listen,
She's like an angel in Heaven, so bright but not always
dressed in white,
I know this girl, I love her so, her name is . . .

Sam Webb (15)
Thomas Keble School

My Uncle

Old days, old ways
Remembering the walk
Christmas time, the soft snow
Beneath our boots
My cousin and I
Having to listen
Having to bear
The sarcasm inside.

Words could not describe
How livid inside
He felt and looked ashamed,
The smell of fresh air
The silent smell of classical
Xmas time food
Only to be spoilt
By someone's personality . . .

James Thorburn (15)
Thomas Keble School

Night Of Dancing

Fire teaser, you demon
Stealing my flames
To warm your chill
Dancing on without my will

Catch me hot embers
Play fight with a fire
Laughing in the falling light
Dance on through this magic night

Silver is the dusk
Glowing is the night
Leap on a fly and ride away
Take my fire, it's dying anyway

Troubles don't burn in the heat of the day.

Brighid Nathanson (15)
Thomas Keble School

The Seaside

Sandcastles being built on the fresh sand
Children standing proudly beside their creation
Then running and screaming with friends
And forgetting all about their sandcastle

Ice cream vans giving their call to children
Hypnotising them to come and eat
Runny ice creams dripping down their tops
Then ends up on the floor anyway

The boats in the distance
Bobbing up and down
On the gentle, calm sea
With gentle cry of seagulls up above

Parents relaxing on the beach
While watching their young play
Nudists burning the eyes of the young
Their flesh burning a salmon pink

The sun sinks like a dead man
The tide destroying creations
One by one deserting the littered sand
Till tomorrow comes.

Jennifer Robinson (15)
Thomas Keble School

A Man Who Smoked

There was an old man
Who smoked a pipe
He slept all day
But snored all night.

> His poor old wife
> Said, 'Don't smoke your pipe
> If you kept busy all day
> You would not snore all night!'

Nathan Robins (13)
Thomas Keble School

It's All Fading Away

Reality is gone,
The only things in sight are random colours and black.

They move randomly in irregular shapes,
They slowly drain into each other.

Yellow, red to blue and purple,
The colours are dancing before your eyes.

This is bliss,
So relaxing yet you can't take your eyes off it.

Reality seeps back into your brain,
You see other things in the room around you.

Move the mouse,
The standard desktop comes back on screen,
Get on with your life.

Don't watch screen savers.

Dave Brook (16)
Thomas Keble School

Uniform

The pupils of this school wear uniform,
The blue and black may seem boring,
Our individuality is calling,
We are made to tuck in shirts to conform.

This uniform is so plain and so dull,
The uniform really, really does stink,
It should be changed a lot I really think,
I hate it so much, we should change in full.

This uniform really, really does suck,
We all want to change it, 'cause it is yuck!

Jo Short (13)
Thomas Keble School

The Little Beach

The strongness of the tide takes the rocks far and wide.
The seagulls play about on the little beach shore.
Way up high in the sky lots of birds start to glide.
The crowds and crowds of people fill up the town galore.
As the tide slowly drifts in and back out,
The sun shines down on the shimmering sea all day.
The little children come to dig and play and shout,
While older people come to tan themselves on the bay.
The little house flashes all night to let the ships go by.
The little boats are tied ashore ready to sail,
And as the day goes by, all the children start to cry.
As the sun sets on the little beach, the boats don't sail.
The little beach begins to quieten for the night,
And can be seen far, far away by sight.

Helena Short (13)
Thomas Keble School

Snake

I am the snake, I move like water
And I lash out like a crocodile
My skin is multicoloured
And camouflaged.

I snake live in the jungle
The jungle is in a lost world
Yet I seem to find my way.

I peel my skin every year
My venom will kill you in a matter of seconds
I have scaly skin
You can call me the snake.

Shannon Poole (11)
Thomas Keble School

Poem About Me

My name is Amy
My hair is brown, my eyes are blue
They are the colour of the ocean I've been told
Deep and dark.

I am twelve years old, almost thirteen
But my parents treat me as if I am three
I enjoy being outside in the fresh air
Letting the wind blow in my hair.

I feel gloomy on Mondays
Remembering I've got five days ahead
Sometimes I feel exhausted by the weekend,
But then I unwind with my friends.

My name is Amy
My hair is brown, my eyes are blue
Now you know all about me
And the things that I like to do.

Amy Bloomfield (12)
Thomas Keble School

Skateboarding

Skateboarding is amazing, it is really fun
We skate all day long, we skate . . . skate . . . skate.
Skateboarding all day long, especially in the sun
Sometimes I bail and sometimes I'm frail.

Some people moan and groan about us skateboarding
But we never give up our favourite sport
No matter what, how much they start complaining
So skateboarding is our favourite sport
And we will always stick to that.

Matthew Edwards (13)
Thomas Keble School

My Dreams!

I dream about . . .
Being able to fly and glide around the clouds,
Being good at sport and coming first,
Getting an A in all of my subjects.

I dream about . . .
Being famous and getting to ride in a limo,
Being an actress in a famous movie,
Giving out autographs to all of my fans.

I dream about . . .
Saving somebody's life,
How scared I would be, but how brave I would feel.

I dream about . . .
What will happen tomorrow?
What has happened today?
What dream will I dream tonight?

As I dream I am fast asleep,
So shhhh,
As I dream again.

Katie Shaylor (12)
Thomas Keble School

Big Wolf

If I were a wolf I'd eat all your meat,
I roam my park like it is my tribe,
Sleeping coldly in the winter,
They play like cubs,
They are evil in the moonlight,
They are as big as the moon.

Chris Ind (11)
Thomas Keble School

Who I Am

I am a boy who likes to . . .

Play guitar,
Watch the tele,
Kick a ball and
Feed my belly.

Do PE,
Play with my mates,
Cook the tea and
Wash the plates.

Do my homework,
Go to bed,
Wake up early,
Because my mum said.

Tyler Ford (12)
Thomas Keble School

Wild Animals

I have two ears,
I eat grass and vegetables,
Farmers hate me,
I live in a burrow,
Who am I?

I'm a rabbit.

I have eight eyes,
Am hairy,
I have eight legs,
I spin webs,
What am I?

I'm a spider.

Joseph Dickenson (12)
Thomas Keble School

Sonnet: That Girl

There's a weird girl at school who knows it all,
Her hair is orange and looks really gay.
She thinks she knows how to play volleyball,
And she always acts out in the school play.

Her brothers are weird just like she is,
Her breath is smelly just like my pet dog.
Her best friend is strange and her name is Liz,
She always hangs out in the girlies' bog.

Can you guess her favourite TV show now?
It is the 'Tweenies' and 'SpongeBob Square Pants'.
But she thinks she's totally cool, how?
But her hobbies are growing wacky plants.

But overall she is my favourite friend,
Even though she drives me round the bend!

Emma Tanner (13)
Thomas Keble School

February/May

February
Clinging winds
Gripping your nose like a cat
On a catnip,
Shivering hands, ears and toes.
Loving hearts from lip to lip.

May
A blaring, hot sun,
A muddle of colours,
Joyous children,
Leaping lambs,
Then it turns into winter,
Miserable days.

Olivia Cole (12)
Thomas Keble School

Who Am I?

I am as silent as a mouse when sleeping,
Kind as a bird caring for its chicks,
Happy and sad like the changing weather.

Who am I?

I am rough when running rugby,
A flash on my bike when racing along,
Tough to beat in a game of tennis.

Who am I?

I am moody in the mornings,
Annoyed when travelling by bus,
Stressed with some school subjects.

Who am I?

I am cared for by my family,
Supported by my friends,
Corrected and taught by teachers.

That is who I am.

Thomas Moore (12)
Thomas Keble School

Love

I looked upon a star tonight
And there you were, shining bright.

I see you come - I see you go,
I see you high - I see you low.

I saw the twinkle in your eye,
It made me want to stop and cry.

I think about what the world would be,
If there were just you and me.

Sophie Denton (13)
Thomas Keble School

A Sonnet About No One

There's a girl at school who thinks she knows it all,
With long black hair and pale skin makes her a witch,
She is skinny because she plays football,
Yeah right, you would not get her on the pitch.
She speaks as if she is the best in class,
She nags like an old granny from a nut house,
She is nothing but a pain in the ass!
She looks like a dead, shrivelled up old mouse,
She walks down the corridor all the time,
She has breath as bad as a rhino's bum,
She can't do the time so don't do the crime,
She hums like a horrible human's bum,
She gives us homework when we don't need it,
Everybody thinks that she did not fit!

Alistair Wood (13)
Thomas Keble School

Fisheye Poem

If I were a fish I would swim upstream,
Jumping through the windy weed.
Changing colour when I can,
Like in winter when it snows.
I would eat all the bugs that
Flooded downstream with their wings so wet.

I am a fish who likes to blow bubbles.
I'm a fish that hides in the rock.
I bury in the mud so I look camouflaged.
Underwater there is no one to boss me around.
I've built a hole in the wall, so now it is time to rest.

Amy Goldstone (11)
Thomas Keble School

My Enemy

This particular woman is called Sam,
Her teeth are wonky, they hang to the side,
Her favourite meal is green eggs and ham,
And if she sat on you, you would have died.

She has a big, chunky beard on her chin,
All around her mouth is a pinkie-red rash,
And her head looks like it's been in a bin,
Face job is needed when she has the cash.

Each side of her face has different sized ears,
Each side of her face has different sized eyes,
You look at her picture and it brings tears,
But tears of funniness in those cries.

I gave you the picture, what do you think?
If I were you now, I'd barf in the sink.

George Taper (13)
Thomas Keble School

Composed In P2

I met a bird down Stratford Park last night
When she spoke her breath smelt like rotten feet
When you saw her she would give you a fright
I would never have taken her down my street
Her lips moved up and down like a goldfish
Her face was so bad she looked like a hag
I never made her her favourite dish
If you were mean she would hit you with her bag
I would never go out in public with her
You could hear her voice from a mile away
Her voice was far from a cat's gentle purr
I hated being with her every hour of every day.

Ryan McGeary (13)
Thomas Keble School

Composed In P2!

The sky is grey as the feelings inside,
Children are running wild on the field,
And the world is calm like children are kind,
Kinder in sorrow as people are killed,
This is what I feel,
This is what I timed,
Where is the love? 'Oh bring it to me,' I plead,
For this is what I see, this is where I line,
All I see is lots of cars that look so fine.
On netball court we play much, much more,
Oh, oh, beware here comes the teacher Mrs Meade,
She'll come and tell me not to mess with the law,
So I guess I'll have to get back on my lead,
So I better not be naughty ever again,
Now I know that thanks to my teacher Mrs Meade.

Kerry Stallon (13)
Thomas Keble School

The Traveller's Truths

Travellers,
Why do you carry the weight of the five men?
What does it matter?

For only one legend will live on,
When all that remains is the memories of the past,
When the legend travels on the breeze,
When the tears for us have been wiped away,
The architect of creation
Shall live on.

Ben Payne (15)
Thomas Keble School

Composed In P2!

(In the style of William Wordsworth's Petrarchan sonnet)

Thomas Keble has nothing to bare,
The council houses stare at me all day,
I see and watch people play,
All the drawings have to be nice and square,
I see the boys playing a football match,
The rude boys shout, 'Get out my way!'
Another boy shouts, 'Or you'll have to pay.'
A football player has a green patch.

The sun is shining as some people play,
Mr Inder walks round the field,
Then Mr Steer does the same all day,
The boy's goalie gloves are worn like a shield,
I hear a girl shout to someone, 'Hey!'
They wave their arms as if a sword they wield.

Sophie Ryan (13)
Thomas Keble School

The Phantom

In the night a phantom grows
To sin upon the people he knows.
Five today, six tomorrow,
This is a phantom that has no sorrow.
In his cave where he lies,
When he goes to sleep, he wishes he could die.
With his cloak of darkness
And inhuman knife skills,
At the speed of lightning another victim he kills.
When the moon and stars will shine,
The phantom will give an unfriendly sign.

Perry Smith (11)
Thomas Keble School

In My Mind . . .

In my mind there is . . .
The rising sun over the Himalayan mountains,
A child's face as she finds money on the pavement,
The swirling colours of flowers in a vase.

In my mind there is . . .
The smile of a mother as she holds her newborn baby,
The feel of cold water as it runs down your throat,
Two countries ending a war that has been going on for decades.

In my mind there is . . .
The sound of music caught on the wind,
The memories of a beloved grandfather,
The feeling you get when you are invited to a friend's birthday.

My mind engulfs sorrow and joy,
Hate and love,
Happiness and anger,
My mind stores special memories that I can remember and smile,
In my mind . . .

Charlotte Lewis (12)
Thomas Keble School

Football

I'm playing football with my friend,
I don't want the game to end.
Oh no! the ball just hit the net,
I might have just lost the bet.

Yes, I just got one back,
Ow! He's trying to hack.
I shot . . . yes it went in the net!
The game's over, I just won the bet.

Callum Churchill (12)
Thomas Keble School

My Beauty

My love has a face like a rubbish tip,
Her eyes glow like a bat and a matchstick.
The black hair grows long above her thick lip,
The nails on her feet are like a sheep tick.
Her voice can be heard in very thick fog,
The nose on her face is such a disgrace.
In fact she smells like a big, hairy dog,
Her feet are so big, they won't win a race.
Her teeth once were white, are now black as soot,
Her long grey hair is like a rabbit's snare.
She walks with a limp upon her left foot,
Only catch her breath if you want a dare.
My love is unique and totally rare,
I will love her forever, even without hair.

Laurie Merchant (13)
Thomas Keble School

Great White Shark

I am a monster,
I eat anything,
I come from Australia.
I hate humans,
I hate bones,
I can smell blood from fifty feet away.
I can chew right through your guts,
I have a big appetite for human flesh.
I can kill a seal in minutes.
I am not afraid of anything,
I am the strongest shark in the world.

Michael McClung (14)
Thomas Keble School

I Am The Dog

I am the dog with the jet-black fur,
Whose energy is second to none.
I am the one whose nose is the wettest,
As if it has been sprayed with a hose a thousand times.
My sense of hearing is so acute, my sense of smell is just the same,
Extremely agile and cute am I, and I love playing outdoor games.

I am the dog with the golden fur,
With the long pink tongue and tail,
I roam the streets searching for meat to keep me alive
In the howling wind and gale.
I visit the forest from whence I came, hunting for game,
I scan the trees,
Shivering cold is all I feel.

I am the dog with the snow-white fur,
I live in an igloo,
Sculpted from ice,
I don't suffer from fleas or lice.
When I sprint along in the snow,
I'm camouflaged from head to toe,
Not even the polar bears know.

We are the dogs,
The best ever three,
Like brothers, are we.

Evie Skinner (11)
Thomas Keble School

If I Were A Cat

If I were a cat I would purr loudly.
If I were a cat I would pounce like a lion.
If I were a cat I would play as if I was as free as a bird.
If I were a cat I would chase my tail as if it was a snake.
If I were a cat I would be a fisherman.
If I were a cat I would sleep like a log.
If I were a cat I would chase mice like they were my only food.

Jack Gyles (12)
Thomas Keble School

Animals

I have two ears,
One nose,
Two eyes,
Brown fur,
Four legs,
A black nose,
I live in a burrow,
I have baby cubs,
What am I?

I am a fox.

I have four legs,
I chase sheep,
I sleep in a kennel,
I am black and white,
My master is a farmer,
What am I?

I am a dog.

Harry Sapsed (11)
Thomas Keble School

Turn Of The Tide

While hatred rules a once peaceful land,
Violence is visible everywhere.
Lost is the love that's been thrown aside,
Now here comes the turn of the tide.

But you will remember,
And I will remember,
The breath before the plunge.

Emma Freeman (13)
Thomas Keble School

The Monkey

I am the monkey swinging in the trees,
I am the monkey with my curly tail.
I am the monkey, agile and swift,
I am the monkey - out of my way.

I am the monkey, friendly and kind,
I am the monkey, clean and neat.
I am the monkey, cheeky as can be,
I am the monkey - out of my way.

I am the monkey, I love bananas,
I am the monkey, elegant and proud.
I am the monkey, cute as can be,
I am the monkey so out of my way.

If ever you find an animal as good as me,
Please tell me, it is your duty.
I'd be very surprised if you ever did,
Because no one is as awesome as *the monkey*.

Miles Lewis-Iversen (11)
Thomas Keble School

Lizzie . . .

Dazzling hair
    Plaited with care.
Dazzling eyes,
    Sparkle as she flies.
Dazzling smile,
    Keeps it as she runs the mile.
Dazzling skin,
    Smooth as paper, quite thin.
Dazzling angel,
    Up in Heaven.

Rosie Conway (11)
Thomas Keble School

Ugly Minger!

His eyes are grey, he never wears jewels,
When he talks he always gobs in our face.
He makes us groan and moan when in the hall
Don't eat what he bakes, it has a bad taste.

With breath like a skunk you're in for a bunk,
His teeth are like a sheet of black paper.
Maybe he is mistaken for a monk,
He always copies us, what a fake.

What does he wear, it looks like underwear,
Call the fashion police, freak on the loose.
Not even tramps would have his hair,
Maybe some energy would give him a boost.

I'm sorry sir, I just have to say . . .
I don't want to see you in that bad way!

Danielle Girdwood (13)
Thomas Keble School

My Sonnet

I met a bird down Stratford Park last night
When she spoke her breath smelt like rotten breath
When you saw her she would give you a fright
I would have never taken her down my street
Her lips moved up and down like a goldfish
Her face was so bad she looked like a hag
I never made her her favourite dish
If you were mean she'd hit you with her bag
When she walked she waddled like a hippo
When she spoke her voice sounded like a squeak
When people laughed at me I said, 'So, so'
When people looked at her they dared to peek
Yes I have finally got rid of her
Her voice was far from a gentle cat's purr.

Sam Reeves (13)
Thomas Keble School

My Identity Is . . .

A global citizen on a dark, dreamy night,
I have a lot of might.
A passport is what I own,
And I like to eat chicken off the bone.

I have quite a pale face,
And I would describe myself as rather ace.
My name is Chris Rice,
And I am nice.

I have big blue eyes,
And I like mince pies.
I have quite small feet
And I am very neat.

I have a big, strong heart,
And I am very smart.
I am small in height,
But I will always put up a good fight.

Chris Rice (12)
Thomas Keble School

Sonnet Number 1

The girl next door thinks she does know it all,
If fat be attractive, she is stunning,
I'll hit her in the head with a football,
I'd hate to see her when she is running,
She has a face only a mum could love,
If hairs be wires, wires grow under her pit,
She is not good enough to own a dove,
I dread seeing her big and mangled bits,
Her lips are fat, dry and have no colour,
Her nails are grubby, dirty, no varnish,
There's no love and no Müller love either,
There's no food around she made it vanish,
Seeing her mangled, dirty, grubby feet,
Not a beauty and not much of a treat.

William Greg (13)
Thomas Keble School

How Many?

How many a brave young man must die?
How many a loving widow must cry?
How long must we wait
For them to understand
That war is a plague that has stricken the land?

How many a killing shot must be fired?
How many years must we linger and grow tired?
How long will it take for them to see
That peace is the way - it is the key?

Tadhg Haydock (13)
Thomas Keble School

War

There's silence around - let the battle commence,
Take your positions, it's all so, so tense.
Bullets flying off in all different courses,
Hitting men riding on horses.
Bodies lying all over the floor,
All of them knocking on death's door.
There's silence around, back once more,
Heaps of dead bodies lie on the floor.

Arthur Milroy (13)
Thomas Keble School

Where Am I?

Where am I?
Am I near or far?
Who am I?
Searching for my past.
What am I?
Just a mere thing in the world.
Why am I here?
To do something important.

Roberta Wilkes (11)
Thomas Keble School

Mrs Meade!

Her nose is crocked like a bent train track,
She dresses like a Goth; she drinks witches' broth.
I would never look at her from the back,
She's so clever she acts like she's a boff.

She's so sneaky; she acts like a detective,
She frightens the whole class with her loud screech.
For her class she is over protective,
She says an A grade is out of reach.

She speaks like a bat; her breath really reeks,
She can't dress to save her life; what a freak!
She never gives us any of her treats,
She stuffs them into her very hungry beak.

But I really like my English teacher,
Even though she's like a freak of nature.

Kerry Stephens & Nathan Scrivens (13)
Thomas Keble School

The Monster!

The hair on her head is like a broom,
Her eyes are dull, nothing like the rainbow.
I hate the smell when she walks in the room,
It's all her fault she stinks of BO.
Her face is so pale, she's as fat as a whale,
Her armpits are hairy and really, really scary.
She drinks far too much ale and she's going stale,
I just found out her name, which is Hairy McLairy.
Her nose is like a witch's toe,
Her teeth are like a sheet of black paper.
I hope I will never see her later,
She is the biggest minger, she can be a right winger.
She is the total opposite to a goddess,
In her room is a massive mess.

Kieran Stanton-Jones (13)
Thomas Keble School

The Nasty Old Man

The sun goes in, the wind stands still as he appears.
Children run to their houses and bolt the doors.
He rambles down the street, the air is filled with fear.
They shriek with fright as they hear footsteps on the floor.

Bellows down the silence in the once joyful street.
If you saw this town you would think it wasn't loved.
It was loved till he came, you would hate to meet him.
Ever since he came, happiness has been shoved.

Parents worry for their kids as he passes by.
Animals run to their homes when they see his face.
He could make some friends, but he doesn't even try.
Children cry, 'Why is this such a terrifying place?'

Poor people dealing with him living in their town.
They know, he knows, I know he'll never live this down.

Gemma Carpenter (13)
Thomas Keble School

As Long As They Rescue Me!

They, the ones who run over animals, let them die a painful death,
What business of mine as long as they come to rescue me.

They, the ones who hit animals by cars,
Leaving them to suffer on the edge of the pavement, howling for help,
What business of mine as long as they come to rescue me.

Every evening when the day comes to close,
Thousands of animals are killed by cars,
Seeing their life end in front of them,
What business of mine as long as they come to my rescue.

And then one day I got hit,
Do you think they will come to my rescue?

Matt Hobbs (14)
Thomas Keble School

My Identity

My parents naming me as I lay by their side,
At playgroup, printing my hand and calling it mine,
My brilliant birthdays, each one always as amazing as the one before,
receiving excellent gifts and having joyful celebrations.

These things make me who I am . . .

My education blossoming successfully over the years,
My language and literacy skills improving every day,
Pieces of work being returned to me with helpful hints and tips,
such as 'use more adjectives' and 'try and find more exciting verbs'.

These things make me who I am . . .

Photos of my family and I having fun and enjoying ourselves,
A video about my old primary school, with my younger self
on the screen,
Little comments and messages from many of my old friends,
wishing me luck in the future, as I start secondary school,
then college, then hopefully a first job.

All of these things make me who I am.

Katharine Birkin (12)
Thomas Keble School

Brothers

My brothers are as bossy as teachers.
My brothers are sometimes as moody as monsters.
My brothers' rooms are very messy.
My brothers are as tall as lamp posts.
My brothers are glued to the telly.
My brothers are very kind, like Santa.
My brothers are very smelly, like a dog.

Gemma Mitchell (11)
Thomas Keble School

Autumn Days

Sleeping, dead trees
The smash of the conker fight
The time of bloody hunting
Goons and ghosts of Hallowe'en
Jack Frost and his silver, sparkling paint
Fireworks crackling and banging in the sky
The harvest coming with bread and wheat and crops
Crunching leaves on the ground
Animals like hedgehogs going to sleep for winter
Little children splashing in the puddles
Rain falling from the cloudy sky
The sun shortening the day
The moon lengthening the night
Time going back an hour.

Jonathan Tuckett (12)
Thomas Keble School

Composed In My English Room

As I stare mindlessly out of the glass
I see the green grass blowing in the breeze
As the PE group stand, begin to freeze.
Small, wet dewdrops glittering in the grass,
I see the sun shining brighter then brass.
As the gusty wind blows into the trees
Thousands and thousands of red and brown leaves fall
And start tip-a-tapping on the glass window
As if they're trying to get in.
I see everything, fields, woods and hills,
The wind blows harder, a yellow bin blows past,
Everything stops, lies still.
It is all very calm and quiet
In Thomas Keble School, all silent until . . .

Rebekah Kay (13)
Thomas Keble School

My Enemy

My enemy has a brain of a pig,
Her glasses bigger than her head is round,
My enemy has the hips of a fig,
Upon her head is a fat, smelly mound.

Short, lumpy, disgusting, hairy, lard legs,
Long, spiky teeth are hanging out of her gob,
When she lifts her arms all you smell is eggs,
When she sits she looks like a big fat blob.

When she stands her stomach sags to the floor,
Her dirty voice is gravelly and hard,
She gets stuck when she squeezes through the door,
What a nasty thing, that's pure lard.

Her grey and murky, milky, muggy eyes,
I don't think she will ever get the guys.

Rachel Montague (13)
Thomas Keble School

Composed In P2

Teachers fussing around the building site.
Children's faces, groaning and moaning.
Looking through the window on Monday morning.
Children at it, it turns into a fight.
As soon as it stops here comes Mr Dwight.
The sad kid goes to tell and starts phoning.
His mum picks him up and starts complaining.
He is back at school all happy and bright.
He goes back to his tutor room P2.
Mrs Meade asks him if he is better.
When he passed a test his confidence grew.
A day off school he gave in a letter.
Time to catch the bus home, the bus is blue.
It's tipping down, I'm getting wetter.

Tyrell Edmond (13)
Thomas Keble School

Autumn Days

Fireworks flying
Crunchy leaves
Long scarves
Conkers cracking
Harvest festival
Wavy wind
Floating leaves
Pumpkins all around
Slippery frost
Frozen water
Cold-looking windows
Cloudy sky
Freezing air
Squeaky squirrels
Booming bonfires
Flying leaves
Dark smoke.

Callum Bonner (13)
Thomas Keble School

Dolphin Kennings

Fish-eater
Bar-jumper
Cool-flipper
Voice-squeaker
Splash-maker
Wave-surfer
Smooth-swimmer
Squid-sucker
Sea-lover
Tail-whipper
Leap-lover.

Jordan Coxhead (12)
Thomas Keble School

Identity

Who is he?
What does my passport say?
Obviously it says I'm me
But who may he be?

I'm a cheeky sort of chappy
Once you get to know me
A kind and caring sort of guy
But don't upset me 'cause I'll punch you in the eye!

Only joking, I'm having a laugh!
'Cause I'm that type of guy
What you see is what you get
I'm really not that sly

Smartly dressed or Mr Scruff
I like to joke around
I may look rough, I may talk tough
But that's just the way I sound

I'm really me, I'm quite unique
Although I look like my brother
I'm quite different in many ways
That's right, I'm like no other.

Sam Westerby (12)
Thomas Keble School

Snake Kennings

Sly-slider
Slick-slitherer
Venom-sprayer
Fang-shower
Windy-wiggler
Mouse-eater
Human-attacker
S-shaper
Skin-shedder.

Josh Jones (12)
Thomas Keble School

Identity!

This is my search to find who I am,
How do I know that I'm different from you?
Does my name change who I am?
Let me see through another's eyes.

Let me know who I am.

I'm trying to find my identity,
Am I the same as anyone else?
Not everyone can be unique can they?
Tell me the answer I need to know.

Let me know who I am.

I'm looking to find how I'm different,
How did I choose who to be?
Why do I get on better with others?
Show me my identity.

How can I tell who's me?

My star sign is Taurus,
I was born in the year of the monkey,
I like drawing and animals,
But there are loads of people like that!

How can I know what I mean?

If I was born a minute earlier than I was
Who would I be?
If I couldn't do the things *I* enjoy,
What would I like to do?

Isabelle Starkiss (12)
Thomas Keble School

Nine-Month Loss

(Based on 'Mid-term Break' by Seamus Heaney)

I sat all morning in my hospital bed,
Counting down the seconds, minutes, hours.
Finally, at two o'clock, my parents drove me, and only me home.

In the porch I met my husband crying -
He had always taken death in his stride -
And his brother saying it was a cruel world.

My little girl raced around the house, laughing,
Not sure what exactly was going on
In her home - why were there so many sad people?

And where was her baby sister she had been waiting for -
For so long - where was she now?
I stood, lost and alone in the middle of my sitting room,

Arm linked with that of my husband
As we hopelessly fought back the stream of angry tears,
When we should be celebrating the birth of our second child.

Instead, mourning the death, she never really lived though
So how could we mourn her death?
At five o'clock, her fragile corpse arrived.

Next morning, I went up to the nursery. Lilly's.
And candles replacing the baby toys we had bought,
I saw her for the second time in my life.

Still, she looked perfect. Still, no noise escaped her.
She lay in her one-foot box, her only cot,
She never slept in one, just my arms, then her box.

A one-foot box, not even a foot for day of life.

Katherine Warner (15)
Thomas Keble School

Match Day

It's match day, the pressure's on,
I have to focus, 3 points to be won.
I sort my kit, get psyched and head towards the ground,
I arrive, meet the lads and get my kit on.

I tie my boots tight, put shoulder guards on and bite my mouth guard.
I jog to the perfect pitch, and take some practise kicks.
I slot the lot, stretch off, now I'm really warm.

It's match day, the pressure's on.

The enemy arrive and inspect the pitch,
They retreat to put their colours on.
Both teams have one last talk,
Their fans talk abuse but I stay quiet,
My hands and feet will retaliate.

It's match day, the pressure's on.

The whistle blows, the ball goes up,
The second row takes it in,
It protected and comes to the back,
No 9 feeds me the ball, I dummy to number 12 and dart inside,
Bang! 40 yards gained, forwards ruck over and ball is out.
'Offside opposition!' shouts ref.
I signal for post as the tee is brought on by mascot Tetley.
Focus, posts. Step back and to the side, eyes on the ball.
Ping, it sails through 3-0.
40 minutes pass and score stays still.

Second half has thunderous hits, blood, red cards,
Dump tackles, the lot,
But we win 13-0,
Converted try and a penalty were added,
Full time,
Pressure's off.
Into the clubhouse for a well earned drink.

Chris Powderly (15)
Thomas Keble School

In My Box

(Based on 'Magic Box' by Kit Wright)

I will put in my box . . .
The music of Nelly
Smoke from my mum's ears
The hard leather of a football.

I will put in my box . . .
The comfort of a hug
The softness of a pillow
The warmth of a fire.

I will put in my box . . .
The laughter of my friends
The joy of my first word
The excitement of films.

I will put in my box . . .
The feelings of winning something
The joy of a team winning, you support
The emotions of leaving primary school.

I will put in my box . . .
The memories of holidays
The memories of family
The memories of friends.

I will put in my box my life.

Charlie Bond (12)
Thomas Keble School

Haiku

Conkers dropping down,
Leaves swirling all around me,
It's cold out here now.

Kate Oboussier (12)
Thomas Keble School

Truck

The skin blackens like black,
There never are enough road crossings.

Imagine the intensity of it,
The large splat, belching
On an open road,
The voice of a kindly god.

Sometimes the sudden choke of air,
The municipal blood bursts.
Body crashes to the ground
And the flow has found a scream of pain.
From the streets, a congregation:
Every newspaper agent and news reporter around butts in,
With cameras, microphones, note pads, beards,
Posh suits,
Frantic hands.

And a flattened man,
Screaming in the liquid sun.
His highlights polished to perfection,
Flashing lights,
And the blessing sings
Over his broken bones.

Steve Roberts (15)
Thomas Keble School

Crash Haiku

She falls down, down, down,
There's silence for a long time!
The sirens are heard.

Emily McCollum (12)
Thomas Keble School

I Am

The skin of Swedish sunlight,
The mystery of a gentleman's puzzle,
A tortoise on a journey,
The note of Beethoven's work,
The drawing of a delicate designer.

I am . . .

The word of a spectacular school child,
The window of a purple house,
The needle in a haystack farm,
The drop in a marine-blue ocean,
The precious glass of a vase.

I am . . .

The petal of lavender,
The work of an amazing artist,
The leaf of a three-leafed clover,
A wonder, a one of a kind,
I am me.

Amanda Engstrom (12)
Thomas Keble School

Who Am I?

Chest-banger
Land-owner
Brill-swinger
Man-primate

Flea-picker
Fruit-eater
Brain-boxers
Mammal-maniac
Land-breather!

Megan Baker (12)
Thomas Keble School

Who Am I?

Who am I?

I am Martin Mills,
An ordinary kid.
I go to Thomas Keble School,
To stuff knowledge in my head.

Who am I?

I have many hobbies,
Like doing magic tricks,
I can pull my finger off my hand,
And make books levitate.

Who am I?

I like spending time with friends,
We like to chat and play.
My friends and I like hanging out,
When we have the time.

Who am I?

Perhaps now you know,
The answer to this question,
Who is Martin Mills,
The ordinary kid?

Martin Mills (12)
Thomas Keble School

September

Mountain of presents,
Weather as cold as ice!
Buckets of rain and drowning flowers,
Leaves as brown as dark chocolate.

Melissa Ridgway (13)
Thomas Keble School

How To Make Lucy Clark

Ingredients:
2 handfuls of hair
A big smile
A dollop of pink
A sprinkle of sweetness
A pair of green eyes
Some crazy ideas
4 tbls of happiness

Method:
Take the 2 handfuls of hair and put in a bowl
Mix well. While you are doing that add a big smile.
Bake. Sprinkle sweetness and add to bowl.
Stir dollop of pink and crazy ideas together,
Add green eyes and 4 tbls happiness.
Cook for 10 minutes and you're done, you have made Lucy Clark!

Lucy Clark (11)
Thomas Keble School

Formentor Beach

The sunny spells on the clear beach blinded my eyes,
As the gritty sand gets in my hair and my toes,
The sunny spells turn into rain, that's all big lies,
The gentle waves glitter and shine, the strong wind blows,
Through my hair, the children's laughs make me giggle, he-he,
They run around making sandcastles and laughing,
The kids get scared because of the big buzzy bee,
The noise of the adults' mobiles go ring-ring,
The smell of the food makes you want to eat, eat, eat,
The cold drinks from the cafe tastes very nice,
The man from the hotel takes my comfy seat,
The beach here is very nice, like sugar and spice,
Most of the time here me and my friend just played,
So overall here I'm just glad I stayed!

Maizey Roberts (13)
Thomas Keble School

Her Life

'It doesn't matter,' she would say
Unwilling to talk
Wanting only to push others away

She was alone, on her own
Never wanted to bother others
Secrets she'd kept to herself for years

Nobody could know how
You, you caused her so much pain
She almost went insane

You changed her so much
From happy and carefree
To depressed and speaking to no one

Like an evil touch she'd changed
Like the seasons, the leaves on the trees
Red-anger, green-calm

But she was yellow and brown leaves
You can't describe them
But they describe her life

'It doesn't matter,' she would say
It mattered
How her life was now shattered.

Clair Akhurst (15)
Thomas Keble School

Newquay

The strength of the waves shatter the big, grey rocks
The heaviness of the tide pushes surfers out
The little waves gradually move along to the docks
From the loudness of the people you have to shout
You're walking round a shop thinking, *wow, I want that top!*
Meanwhile outside people are queuing to have a snack
Carrying on down the street I spot another shop
But then I realise I have to start to pack!

Carly Woodward (13)
Thomas Keble School

London

In the depths of London, rats, other small rodents.
The smell from nearby rubbish tips fill the air around.
When Big Ben rings for noon there are twelve single moments
And time stands still and there is not a single sound.
Fumes that fill the air will make your snot turn blackish!
The homeless people on the street, begging for food.
It really makes you quite depressed, it's sort of saddish.
Children down the street will be egging, being rude.
Dark, damp places make you want to cringe. Roadside kills.
Underground tubes becoming loose, also are death traps.
People having lots to drink and taking lots of pills.
Lager, beer, vodka, shots, all of these and schnapps.
But on the outskirts of London happy people,
Not polluted, but diluted happy people . . .

James Hopkins (13)
Thomas Keble School

How To Make Lisa Brown

Ingredients:
One great big smile.
Two great big wheels.
A sprinkle of talent.
Two brown eyes.
A chunk of brown hair.
5kg of moodiness in the mornings.
25kg of cherry cola
One half of a pound of humour.

Method:
Firstly take one great big smile
and a sprinkle of talent in her brain.
Next sprinkle 5kg of moodiness in the morning
and a half a pound of humour then stir in 25kg of cherry cola.

Lisa Brown (11)
Thomas Keble School

The Earth

I'm losing faith in all humankind
Collapsing under the lack of trust that I find.

The sort that bubbles and brews inside
Hatred that's hard to cover and hide.

Feelings so deep and emotions concealed
Scars on our souls that will never be healed.

We need to take hold of the world in its races
And stop committing so many disgraces.

We destroy the beauty that we behold
There's so much history that hasn't been told.

Who needs to know about nature and the world?
When we've a wad of twenties so crisp and so curled.

One day the Earth will get fed up and sigh
And that will be it. Mankind will die.

Megan Warren (15)
Thomas Keble School

Friendship

Friendship is a precious gift
A bond shared between two people
It's a strong chain of energy
Full of laughs and tears
Excitement and fears
A journey with companionship
Dragged through mental bogs
And sunny times
Friendship is a personality shaping
And character making
Friendship is a precious gift.

Yssy Baker (15)
Thomas Keble School

How To Make Jenny Adams

Ingredients:
I big smile
5 handfuls of mud
3/4 of a cup of determination
2 scraped knees
10 handfuls of curly hair
A dollop of happiness
5kg of laughter
1 crazy body

Method:
Firstly put 1 big smile and 5kg of laughter into a bowl
And carefully stir until the smile has dissolved.
Next add 3/4 of a cup of determination and a dollop of happiness.
Now add the 10 handfuls of curly hair,
2 scraped knees and 5 handfuls of mud.
Stir all the ingredients together, and then add 1 crazy body.
Finally leave the mixture to cool for 24 hours
And then Jenny Adams will be set.

Jenny Adams (12)
Thomas Keble School

How To Make Emily Nobes

Ingredients:
A handful of footballs
2 brown eyes
Some slightly red hair
1 sprinkle of 'SpongeBob Squarepants'
A cup of laughter.

Method:
Take two brown eyes and some slightly red hair, and slightly stir until
thin.
Chop up a few footballs and carefully sprinkle over the thin mixture.
Chuck in a 'SpongeBob Squarepants', and bake until golden brown.
Then finally serve with chocolate ice cream.

Emily Nobes (11)
Thomas Keble School

How To Make Georgia Wood

Ingredients:
1 big smile
A room full of dogs
Many bad jokes
5 tablespoons full of whacko ideas
A dollop of purple
4 big scrapes of brownie-blonde hair
A scrape full of lyrics and dancing scenes.

Method:
Take 1 big smile and put in mixing bowl,
And mix it with many bad jokes.
After, stir with a whisk,
Then throw in a room full of dogs
And mix with a dollop of purple.
When the dogs are purple,
Scrape 4 big handfuls of brownie-blonde hair,
And then mix together again.
When you have finished that,
Rinse 5 tablespoons full of whacko ideas
And mix with a scrape full of lyrics and dancing scenes,
Then put into the oven for 40 minutes.

Georgia Wood (11)
Thomas Keble School

A Shoal Of Fish

A shoal of fish is a group of shiny pennies in a wishing well,
A burst of stardust in a black sky,
A pulse of light from a submarine deep down,
A patch of dots on a blank page.

A shoal of fish moves like silver bullets in a dark blue sky,
Like a handful of diamonds thrown over a sandy beach,
Like blue butterflies high in the sky.

Hayden Scamp (11)
Thomas Keble School

War Or Peace?

Peace is a colourful flower,
Blooming in the stark cold of winter.
It is a mother's love,
Spreading happiness.
Peace is friendship,
Never breaking, always together.

Peace is life!

War is pitch-blackness,
Rolling over and over swallowing up the moon.
War is hot anger,
Ripping up everything around it.
It is an angry bull,
Causing devastation.

War is death!

Shona Corbett (11)
Thomas Keble School

Dog Sonnet

Two creatures that descend from snarling grouped monsters,
Which run at the pace of hunting or hunted wind,
Beasts with IQ below the level of tricksters,
Tearing out stuff that has recently just been binned,
Constantly lazing about on the new sofa,
Blurs of black and yellow just when dinner is served,
Shedding hairs in the car with their human chauffeur,
Barking, pulling and snarling when something just purred,
Always fighting each other with jaws round the neck,
Obediently doing tricks for tasty treats,
Getting excited because they're having a trek,
Being friendly or nasty to a dog who meets,
They could just be thought of as the hounds of the hells,
But they are really just dogs and being themselves.

Joe Jenkins (13)
Thomas Keble School

The Destruction

In the corner of my room, I've seen death,
I've also seen families fall apart
And worst of all destruction to the world.

In the corner of my room, I've seen the world
Haunted by hurricanes and tornadoes,
Consuming the world bit by bit,
Destroying lives and homes.

In the corner of my room, I've seen children
Haunted by adults, kept hostage
Sitting in fear,
Waiting to be released or die.

In the corner of my room, I've heard screams
Of death, sirens eating any noise,
I've heard the world cry for help.

Television.

Hannah Chappell (11)
Thomas Keble School

A War Poem

How much would it cost,
A perfect society
With freedom and peace?

No more war or hate?
No more death or killer bombs
And no more hunger?

With love and delight?
With happiness and pleasure?
With joy and no hate?

How much would it cost,
A perfect society?
But does it exist?

Lara Crook (13)
Thomas Keble School

If I Were A Cat

If I were a cat
I would sleep in the grass,
And chase mice.

If I were a cat
I would cuddle up to my owner,
Like a teddy in a child's arms.

If I were a cat
I would watch the sunset and sunrise,
It would be like watching fire.

If I were a cat
I would sit in front of the fire in winter,
To move me it would be like taking a bone from a dog.

If I were a cat
I would play in the long grass on a summer's day,
To find me it would be like finding a needle in a haystack.

If I were a cat
I would explore the street,
And be back in time for tea.

Katie-Lousie Churchill (11)
Thomas Keble School

My Chinchilla Wilson

Wilson is like a kangaroo jumping everywhere
Wilson runs as fast as a cheetah in the windy air

Wilson is a cool dude swanking in the breeze
Wilson likes lots of food but doesn't like cheese

Wilson is like a snowball rolling down a hill
Wilson runs up the wall and on the window sill

Wilson is a loner, but likes it by himself
Wilson gets attention by rattling on his shelf

Wilson is my favourite pet in the whole wide world!

Harley-Ray Hill (11)
Thomas Keble School

The Dog

I could hear howling and whining noises
Every day and night.
Then I could hear no noise
Looking out the window
I saw the dog going for a walk
Without a lead
The owner following it
What business of mine is it?

One night in the winter
Looking out the window
I saw the dog
No lead
No owner this time
What business of mine is it?

Skinny, but very weak
It was limping
Then collapsed
What business of mine is it?

I saw the owner
He didn't look worried
He put his hand on it
What business of mine is it?

I could see that it was alive
But he just booted it
Then left it to die in pain
What business of mine is it?

He got his car
Stuffed the dog in the boot
He drove off
What business of mine is it?

Jess Hendy (15)
Thomas Keble School

Isaac McMorrow Recipe

Ingredients:
Mixing bowl of freckles.
Big fry up.
2 footballs.
A dollop of excitement.
2 tablespoons of madness.
7 Red Hot Chilli Pepper albums.
A box of Oxo Cubes.

Method:
Take mixing bowl of freckles
And add big fry up and dollop of excitement.
Bake until hard.
Cut hole in the middle of the mixture
And insert two footballs.
Place Red Hot Chilli Pepper albums next to footballs.
Crush Oxo Cubes and sprinkle on top of the substance
Then add 3 tablespoons of madness.
Mash substance together then fry.
Leave for two hours then ready.
When cooked serve big fry up to make him happy.

Isaac McMorrow (12)
Thomas Keble School

The Baby

The baby is cute and cuddly
He rolls around on the floor happily
The baby starts to cry
To make you upset he howls
Like an owl at night
Then he sleeps soundly
Dreaming of Heaven
As soft as a woolly lamb
In his white blanket.

Megan Laws (11)
Thomas Keble School

My Magic Box

(Based on 'Magic Box' by Kit Wright)

A vial of venom from a deadly snake,
A drop of colour from the sky,
An apple of infinite sweetness,
Plus a bough from the eldest oak.

A CD containing my music labours,
The sound of water tinkling,
A nice big coconut (just in case)
And a veil of blue silk.

A flask of bitterness,
And another of gratitude,
A bronze fist . . .
And the hand of friendship.

I shall take these precious relics,
And place them in a box,
Made from sky-iron,
And gilded with gold,
And with a lock as solid as the foundations of the Earth.

I shall bury it in an orchard,
With a river running by,
And leave it there until the end of time,
As a living memory.

Richard Townsend (12)
Thomas Keble School

In The Night

The night is an endless black sheet
With twinkling spots of light.

The night is a block of darkness
Covering the bright sun.

The night is when the sun blows out
And the moon comes out.

Ashley Kent (11)
Thomas Keble School

How To Make Hannah Bucknell

Ingredients:
1 Handful of neatness
A sprinkle of sneezes
10 episodes of 'Friends'
10 tablespoons of determination
5kg of kindness
2 dollops of happiness
1 heart for family
1 heart for friends
A very weird character
5kg of madness

Method:
Firstly take 5kg of madness
and mix together well with 10 episodes of 'Friends'
and sprinkle the sneezes over it.
Next scrape a handful of neatness
and 10 tablespoons of determination.
Then put 1 heart for family and 1 heart for friends
and kneed everything together.
Place the very weird character
and 2 dollops of happiness
and stir until you get a pink coloured mixture.
Put in the oven for 10 minutes at 250°c.

Hannah Bucknell (11)
Thomas Keble School

My Dog Toby

My dog Toby is as cute as a baby,
He is a puffball of soft fur.
My dog is as silly as Goofy,
My dog is as friendly as the Queen.
My dog has a tail of surrender.
He is a fussy, playful dog
And he is the centre of the family.

Darren Brocklehurst (11)
Thomas Keble School

My Identity

Pictures of my mom and me playing and joking,
My sister laughing at me choking,
The first cheese sandwich with my gramp.

That's what made me.

Santa's footsteps in my bedroom,
Jumping in puddles with my pink wellies,
Dreaming I was a fish swimming in the sea.

That's what made me.

Fairy wishes coming true,
First injury I ever had,
First word my cousin spoke.

That's what made me.

My life is bright and colourful,
With my friends and family by my side,
I have good days and bad days,
But I can't hide.

I shall live my life as if it's my last day,
Go to America and model,
My dreams will come,
I'll make them.

That is what will make me.

Shannon Absalom (13)
Thomas Keble School

My Dog Is . . .

My dog is as grumpy as an angry man.
My dog's teeth are like a can opener.
My dog's ear is like a cat flap.
My dog eats like an old man.
My dog's eyes are as if it is crying.
My dog protects me like a big bodybuilder, my bodyguard.
But after all I've said, it is my dog and I love him altogether.

Jordan Day (11)
Thomas Keble School

Road Kill Cafe

Badger burger
Mushy fleas
Spring vole
Sausage mole
Snail spaghetti
Munk flurry
Gutted goose
Diced mice
Dead dog
Cat crunches
Kitten ketchup
Tread turtle
Slug soap
Snake salad
Butterfly biscuits
Bat bacon
Rundown rabbit
Fishy faggots
Fried eel
How about a meal?

Sam Underwood (13)
Thomas Keble School

My Caterpillar

My caterpillar is a gleaming ruby,
My caterpillar is like a zombie that rises from the dead.
My caterpillar is like a pig,
My caterpillar is a slimy, small dragon.

My caterpillar is a bodybuilder,
My caterpillar is as slow as a tortoise.
My caterpillar is a fat bee,
My caterpillar is an Olympic champion.

John-Paul Crawford (11)
Thomas Keble School

Don't They Think Of Everyone In The World

All these major powers,
Competing in the space race.
They spend billions and billions,
On tiny space probes.
Don't think of everyone in the world?

All those people that are poor,
In India, Africa and Sudan.
Imagine what it would be,
If they had a billion.
They would have food, homes and clothes.
Don't they wish for everything in the world?

Wouldn't it be great,
To have equality.
Everyone well off,
Not anyone that's poor.
Maybe that's the way it has to be.
Nobody knows.

Jimmy Bower (13)
Thomas Keble School

War

USA troops all over the city,
We give them all lots of pity.
Machine guns clunking in my ear,
I do fear.

Bombs have been hurled,
All over the world.
People are dying,
Please stop trying.

Gunshots I hear repeating,
How I fear them defeating.
Loud banging in my ear,
Trying hard to stop my fear.

Sophie Kerry (13)
Thomas Keble School

My Poem

I will sit and have a fag
In the latest Jag
So when I am sixty-four
And lying dead on the floor
Yes, that makes me really cool.

When I smoke twenty a day
Kill the Earth in every way,
Because smoking produces 10 times more
Than driving down the M4
Pollution's great - it's first rate.

Yay, I'm doped up once again,
But I can't remember how, why or when.
Hallucinations are really cool.
There's chickens on the nightclub floor,
Yeah, I'm the man!

Jack Marshall (13)
Thomas Keble School

My Spanish Villa

The sun shines onto the breaking walls
The telly blasts through the abandoned house
There is no one here, no one at all
It's all so quiet, as quiet as a mouse
The outside glistens, especially the pool,
The sun's beaming down, heating up everything
It's sometimes hot, but sometimes cool
I wish there was something to do here, anything
At night the town and people come alive
The fireworks boom and the bright lights glow
In the streets the adults and children jig and jive
When the night ends you know the good feeling has to go
As I lie here, thinking over what I have done today,
I know tomorrow will be okay.

Angharad England (13)
Thomas Keble School

Millions Die Just For Fun

A war of the countries, a war of the lands,
A war for the sea and a war for the sands,
A bigger country firing guns,
Millions die just for fun.

A war for the weapons, a war for the power,
A war to make sure that only one team towers,
So that millions die every day
And why is it them who have to pay,
Innocent children of a third world place,
It is their own blood they have to taste,
So that stronger countries laugh and be dumb
And so millions die just for fun.

A war to show who is the best,
A war to show who is worth less,
But shouldn't we all be equal and the same?
And surely no one should be in pain,
A bigger country makes a small one run,
All so millions die just for fun.

Gabriel Raeburn (13)
Thomas Keble School

Day And Night

Day
It needs . . .
A bright yellow sun, like yellow Smarties and Skittles
White fluffy clouds, like cotton wool balls
Bright green grass, like it's been drawn with a green highlighter
Tall growing trees, like they've been stretched from top to bottom.

Night
It needs . . .
A black sky that is painted on top of the pale blue sky
A silvery moon, as round as a ten pence that has been splattered
                                        with white icing sugar
Bright yellow stars, that look like diamonds, with yellow lights on inside.

Christine Irving (12)
Thomas Keble School

How To Make Lucy Wise

Ingredients:
1 cheesy grin.
5 heaped tablespoons of fun.
A sprinkle of neatness.
1 handful of excitement.
2 bouncy dogs.
Half a cup of determination.
3 scoops of happiness.
A drizzle of friendship.
A pinch of impatience.

Method:
Firstly put 5 heaped tablespoons of fun
And 1 handful of excitement in a bowl,
Let it simmer for 3 minutes.
Then stir well.
Carefully add a sprinkle of neatness while stirring.
Add one cheesy grin and 3 scoops of happiness.
Let it cool down until a slight green colour.
Next chuck in 2 bouncy dogs
Then stir well till smooth and creamy.
Bit by bit sprinkle in half a cup of determination.
Then add one pinch of impatience.
Heat till a pink colour.
Lastly add a drizzle of friendship.

Lucy Wise (11)
Thomas Keble School

How To Make December

December needs . . .
Plated snow like the layers of a chocolate cake.
Crisp, frozen plants like a still image.
Glow from the logs on a raging fire.
The dead leaves eliminated to extinction.

Henry Walker (12)
Thomas Keble School

It's Not My Business

(A poem in the style of Niyi Osundare)

They picked him up the morning before school
Beat him like a stuffed doll
And kicked him to the ground like a football.
                    It's not my business
                    Why should I care?

The next day came
They booted and punched a different guy this time
And made him yell and scream
They all had a punch as if he were a punch bag.
                    It's not my business
                    Why should I care?

Walking to school one early morning
To find her books and belongings had gone, had gone
No clues, nothing to show where they were
Just an empty bag left on the back of a clueless girl.
                    It's not my business
                    Why should I care?

Then one day
As I went to school
A voice was shouting at me
They hit me to the fierce looking ground
Waiting, just waiting for me to fall.

Amy Holder (14)
Thomas Keble School

Limerick

There was a young boy called Foster
Who lived in a place called Gloucester
He fell off a building
The landing killed him
And that was the end of Foster.

Jay Newman (12)
Thomas Keble School

A Life Of A Dog - Kennings

Cat scarer,
Mean thing,
Dribble chops,
Big tongue,
Waggle tail,
Lazy thing,
Deep sleeper,
Good fighter,
Fast runner,
Ball fetcher,
Baby scarer,
Child lover,
Playful dog,
Sharp teeth,
Muddy paws,
Nice walker,
Children's pet.

Sean Box (12)
Thomas Keble School

Skateboarding

Tony Hawk rides the ramps and gets big air
Gliding on his skateboard really fast
In the wind blows his hair
He's won a lot of medals in the past
He does big flips and fat tricks
He does big spins and a massive grind
When sometimes he bails he hurts his spine
He manuals along the floor
He wears cool clothes and trendy shoes
In competitions as gets sick scores
He hangs round with his cool crew
Filming is great, you catch great flicks
When editing the films there's a lot of good pics.

Jake Rogers (13)
Thomas Keble School

Grumpy Old People

They complain that all we eat is junk food
But they don't know what they are on about
They always make us want to scream and shout
And they always say we are so rude.

We have to speak louder so they can hear
Then they explain to us they are not deaf
When they are arguing we are the refs
When they start to shout we quiver with fear.

I wish they would treat us with more respect
And stop talking to us like we are thick
They point at us with their long walking sticks
When you lie they instantly suspect.

But I suppose most old people do care
And always think about child welfare.

Darien Jones (14)
Thomas Keble School

The Old Building

In a big city, in an old abandoned street
Stood a building so rotten, the rats wouldn't even stay
If you stepped in, the walls would fall around your feet
The ceiling tiles were mouldy and full of decay.
There were herds of cockroaches and hundreds of flies
Buzzing around and hiding under old floorboards
The furniture was as grey as the polluted skies
Dust clouds rising, choking - coming in hoards and hoards.
So pathetic, it's not good enough to knock down
Dwelling in the memory of its once splendour
So the house that once stood in the old abandoned town
With the crumbling walls standing forever.
Along with the cockroaches crawling round the floor
It will stand quiet and lonely for evermore.

Rhianne Banyard (13)
Thomas Keble School

The Cat Man

In my house,
As free as a mouse.
As a cat,
With a hat,
With a guy called Pat.
In my house,
As free as a mouse.

I'm as smiley
As Kylie
On a stage
With a page,
In a cage,
I'm as smiley
As Kylie.

Walking down the street
Out came Pete
With his ball
And over the wall,
Ever so tall
Walking down the street
Out came Pete.

Joshua Todd (12)
Thomas Keble School

My Cat Is . . .

Kiwi my black cat is a baby, wailing to be loved and cuddled.
My cat Kiwi is a lion stalking round, waiting for prey.
My cat is a black witch, casting a spell on us.
She is a hypnotist mesmerising us with her cute, slanting eyes.
Kiwi is a murderer, killing innocent mice.
My black cat is a black bull, raging round the house.
She is the moon, staring at our sleeping house.
My black cat Kiwi is my friend, staying round the night forever.

Laura Ruther (11)
Thomas Keble School

By The Stream

By the stream there is silence, it is so quiet.
The water trickles over the moss covered rocks.
It is so peaceful you will never find a riot.
You will find drinking from the stream the bright red fox.
The water is so clear you can see the bottom.
You will see your reflection down in the soft stones.
The stream is so soft to the touch, it's like cotton.
The stream is so old it may have seen many bones.
The tree leans over like a lingering shadow.
The fallen trees, rotting in the moist atmosphere.
The stream goes at its own speed, gently and slowly.
The woods surrounding the stream are filled with wild deer.
The wind rustles through the leaves, then it sounds like chimes.
This is the best place to sit and relax sometimes.

Laura Bellamy (13)
Thomas Keble School

Surfing Sonnet

Occi Ocupello is surfing king,
He rides good waves like no one I've ever seen.
Pushing his board up the waves he makes them sing.
He holds himself with pride, moving so clean.
He lies on his board waiting, waiting, *Jaws.*
On Sunset Beach searching for the monster.
Meeting the beast he bends the gravity's laws.
He takes the crest, focused, as Neptune stirs.
Buzzing, adrenaline flowing through him.
He slides from the top into super blue.
Snaking curves, forcing his aching back limb.
Finally, let go, he knew it was true.
Comes up on the beach holding his board high.
A salute of thanks to gods of surf sky.

Rowan Le Sage (13)
Thomas Keble School

Uniform

The pupils of this school wear uniform,
The blue and black and white may seem boring,
Our individuality is calling,
We are made to tuck in shirts to conform.

This uniform is so plain and dull,
I hate this uniform, it is rubbish,
It may be bulky but not like a bull,
I hate this uniform, it is so smelly.

The uniform is really horrible,
When we came to school we all look the same,
We don't get to show off our sense of fashion,
We all look the same and this is a shame.

This uniform does really, really suck,
We all look and feel like stupid ducks.

Jennifer Corbally (13)
Thomas Keble School

A Perfect World

In the perfect world would we all be happy?
In the perfect world would we all be sad?
A perfect world - would it work?

In the perfect world would there be drugs?
In the perfect world would there be alcohol?
A perfect world - would it work?

In the perfect world would there be murder?
In the perfect world would there be suicide?
A perfect world - would it work?

In the perfect world would there be crime?
In the perfect world would we all stay fine?
A perfect world - would it work?

Jack Wetson (13)
Thomas Keble School

Football

Football is the best sport in the whole world
Zinadine Zidane is my best player
He scored a great goal for France, it was curled
Zidane went home to read a prayer.

England lost and Sven was extremely cross
In the game Beckham was extremely lame
When Henry broke through you know it's a loss
When France scored a second goal it's the game

When the whistle went France shouted with glee
England needs to improve on their fitness
The crowd heard it so they went like a flea
Wayne Rooney needs to lose some flabbiness

I love footy, it's the best,
It's better than all the rest.

Ben Jones (13)
Thomas Keble School

My Dog

My dog is lovely, she's like a mum
But sometimes she doesn't come
When I call her name out loud
She doesn't make a sound.

She has times when she goes mental
But sometimes she's quite gentle
She has lots of energy
And she cleans herself carefully.

When we go for our long walks
She comes over to me and talks
She is lovely, I love her to bits
I will love her forever.

Sophie Dewhurst (11)
Thomas Keble School

School Uniform

The pupils of this school wear uniform.
The blue and black and white may seem boring.
Our individuality is calling!
We are made to tuck in shirts to conform.

These clothes are way too expensive to wear.
The clothes I can enjoy are much cheaper.
The colours I would wear are much deeper.
In the playground I like to look more rare.

The school uniform is not very warm.
The school trousers are virtually bare.
They are not what I would choose to wear.
Our T-shirts are easily torn to shreds.

But uniform can sometimes be comfy
It's better than uniform for PE.

Jethro Lampitt (13)
Thomas Keble School

I Am Fighting For . . .

I am fighting for my country.
I am fighting for my king.
I am fighting for my family.
I am fighting for my kin.
I am fighting for my friends.
I am fighting for myself.
I am fighting for my own free will.
I am not fighting for the wealth.
I am fighting for my honour.
I am fighting for truth.
I am fighting for my companions
And I hope that they are too.

Mitchell Tudor (13)
Thomas Keble School

A Perfect World

In a perfect world,
Nobody cries, screams or shouts.
Nobody fights or blows things up.
Everywhere, there is peace.

In a perfect world,
Nobody is homeless.
Nobody dies of starvation
And everybody is happy.

In a perfect world
There is no terrorism.
Thee is no war.
There is only peace.

In a perfect world,
There is happiness and enjoyment.
There is love that surrounds children.
That is a perfect world.

Sara Sharp (13)
Thomas Keble School

The Sun

The sun is like a gift.
It's a bright light,
It's a ball of fire,
It's a smoking furnace,
It's a huge flame-thrower waiting to burn.

The sun is always smiling,
The clouds are hunting the sun.
It's a fierce animal,
It's racing away from the sun.
The clouds capture the sun,
The sun's gone for the night.

George Price (11)
Thomas Keble School

The Pass

Something feels right
Something is different
Different from the previous
Here it comes.

Looking over the top of the nose
The leading car's wing
A metre or so away
Looming in large.

The wheel
It knows a vast knowledge
And the important information
You're flat in seventh.

Closer and closer
Invisible forces are at work
Slipstreaming, the car sinks behind
As if it were being towed.

Here comes the corner
A cut as sharp as a razor
As you pull out to move alongside
The other car.

Demon late breaking
Hacksaw steering
Slicing through the other driver's line thickly
Back on the power.

The radio in your car
Erupts in pleasure
You passed the leader.

Theo Durrant (15)
Thomas Keble School

Equality

Baby or toddler,
Child or teenager,
Adult or OAP,
We are all equal.
Male or female,
Pink or brown
White or black,
We are all equal.
Green or blue,
Orange or yellow,
Any other colour,
We are all equal.
From the USA,
Europe or Asia,
USSR or Africa,
We are all equal.
South America or Antarctica,
Anywhere at all
In the world,
We are all equal.
Living in a
Mansion or on streets,
Flat or villa,
We are all equal.
Age, colour, sex,
Place of birth,
Or social status,
Do not matter
In this world.
Do they?

Clare Fickling (13)
Thomas Keble School

McDonald's

McDonald's is greasy and rubbish,
The food they serve you is really bad,
It makes me feel really, really, very mad.
It is really bad and makes you quite tubbish.

The menu at McD isn't very long:
Burger, French fries, it's up to you what you take.
All washed down by a soda and a shake.
It's cheap and cheerful, so what could go wrong?

Too many visits can make you obese,
It's time to give up the big triple McC.
No veg in sight, the vitamins you lack,
It's no good, your waistline needs to decrease.

Have a balanced diet every day,
Have a salad to keep burgers away.

Alistair Raghuram (13)
Thomas Keble School

Holidays

Camping in the gales
I love most
Saw a barn owl
Sitting on a post
Walking on the cliffs
Through the gorse so tall
Seals are swimming
Up tails all
Cycling in the woods
And swimming in the sea
Eating Cornish pasties
For my tea.

Tom Leech (12)
Thomas Keble School

An Eye For An Eye

An eye for an eye,
War and peace,
Happiness shimmer,
The war that never sleeps.
From the youngest baby boy
To the oldest crinkled man,
People dying.

War all over the world,
Near, far and now.
The heat of Africa
To cold, chilling bit of Iceland.
From the smallest girl to the oldest woman,
Thousands dying.

Through the ages there's been war,
Swords to guns, we've seen it all!
A high mountain of raging love and hope,
But in a world of hate.
Everyone will die one day,
Let it be in peace.

Stephanie King (13)
Thomas Keble School

Monty

He's a bundle of soft and cuddly grey.
Leaping at everything that moves in his way.
He thinks he's so brave when he leaps at a fly
And lets out a fierce but miniature cry.
He sets a leaf from behind a tree
Then makes a dash but his prey goes free.
He gracefully pounces to grab his toy,
Then slides on the tiles like a boisterous boy.
He loves a cuddle and lots of fuss,
He really is an adorable puss!

Gemma Scotting (12)
Thomas Keble School

Blood Angels

I ran into battle,
It was just a big rattle,
I have a frown
And shot an orc down.

So its grave was on the field,
We were brave and we killed.
I got the flag and held it above my head,
Below me I could see the dead.

After the chase
We ran back to base,
Down came the reinforcements
Upon the battlements.

For evermore
We stood tall.

Adam Pinkney (11)
Thomas Keble School

Sunshine

You make me very happy
You make me feel warm
I like the different colours
Of your shining face.

At times you look red
At times you look yellow
At times you look orange
Sometimes you are even on fire.

I don't understand why
You have to go,
But I just can't wait
Until you shine again next year.

Laura Wilkes (12)
Thomas Keble School

My Penny

I found a magic penny,
I thought my life was good,
I first wished I knew everything,
But my friend said I was too good.
My second wish was
I did not have to go to school,
In the end I wanted
To go even more.
My third and last wish
Was I could stop time,
But as I got older,
My friends stayed the same.
I chucked the penny
In the sea,
Never to be seen again
By me.

Matthew Austin (11)
Thomas Keble School

No More School

If school were abolished
I would be the happiest boy alive.
No more work or exercise books,
I put them in demise,
No more text books or tests,
For that would be best.
If there was no more school
I could take a rest.

No more teachers to tell you what to do
They keep you in when you really need the loo.

Kyle Summers (12)
Thomas Keble School

Woody Of The Wood

Woody of the wood
Gave a sorrowful sigh
As his poor owner
Tried not to cry.

Asked by people
If OK,
He simply nodded
And walked away.

Woody of the wood,
Shaken with fear
As his poor owner
Shed millions of tears.

Until the day
He came to me,
I began to feel sorry
As the dog was tied to a tree.

But there was a good ending
For Woody of the wood,
He did what wanted,
He did what he could.

Jamie Hobbs (11)
Thomas Keble School

Poetry

I went out to catch some fish
With my maggots in my dish
I took my basket and my rod
A man walked past and gave me a nod

I sat on the bank and set up my stuff
I looked in the sky and the weather looked rough
I looked at the sky and started to groan
I packed up my stuff and walked on home.

Michael Trinder (13)
Thomas Keble School

Why Must I Die?

Why must I die here in my bed?
I did nothing wrong
In my existence here in this world.
I loved,
I gave,
I worked hard.
Why me?
Why now?
When will I go?
Where will I go?
I'm scared,
I'm cold,
I'm worried,
I'm . . .

Ben Poole (13)
Thomas Keble School

The Pig

I am the fattest animal in the world,
I am a big, fat pig.
My feet are like small logs.
I come from a sty,
I smell like rotted eggs.
I am like a big round ball.
I like my food a lot.
I like people looking at me.
I am a rough pig,
I like playing in the mud.
I have pink skin.
I do not want to be killed.
People eat me on a Sunday with gravy.

James Humphreys (13)
Thomas Keble School

An Animal Alphabet Poem

A ligator - adventurous, arrogant
who is boring and lazy.

B ear - big, brave
who always runs and never keeps still.

C at - clever, caring
who has a big, long tail and always shows off.

D og - determined, defeatless
who are loyal and who have very soft coats.

E lephants - enormous, extra strong
who eat all the time and sing all day long.

F rog - fast, furious
who sits on a rock and plays the guitar.

G iraffe - glee, great
who has a very long neck and talks all the time.

H ippopotamus, hideous, heroic
who has very strong arms and never has a bath.

I guana - idiotic, irresponsible
who never moves and has a green, long tail.

J aguar - jealous, jittery
who hunts for its prey and eats them rapidly.

K iller whale - keen, kind
who plays with his friends and always smiles.

L eopard - lucky, lazy
who has no friends and is never happy.

M onkey - mysterious, mad (crazy)
who swings from tree to tree and eats nothing but bananas.

N octurnal bird - naughty, nice
who flies through the sun and watches TV.

O ctopus - odd, obviously strong
who never smiled and never spoke.

P anda - pathetic, positive
who was a mean bully and hated everyone.

Q uilla Qualla - quick, quiet
who always went shopping and spent lots of money.

R abbit - rude, resistable
who never went to work and lived in a shed.

S nake - sly, smooth
who was a maths teacher and loved his job.

T iger - terrifying, trouble
who is a vegetarian and never eats meat.
U nicorn - unfaithful, unreliable
who went to bed and never got up.
V enomous spider - vicious, voluntary
who always littered and never cared.
W hale - wonderful, weird
who was a genius and always worked hard.
X -ray elephant brain - xenophobia, Xmas mad
who always cried because he was being bullied.
Y ellow - mellow - young yeti
who hated school and never went there.
Z ebra - zombie, zoology
who was always with his girlfriend and loved her a lot.

Sophie Ash (11)
Thomas Keble School

The Magic Box

(Based on 'Magic Box' by Kit Wright)

I will put in my box . . .
The *sight* of a guardian bear in the Canadian snow
I will put a Caribbean beach and the turquoise water.

I will put in my box . . .
The *smell* of car diesel
And the *smell* of men's deodorant.

I will put in my box . . .
The *feel* of car tyres
And the *feel* of ice melting in my hand.

I will put in my box . . .
The *taste* of juicy raspberries
With their sour sharpness
And the *taste* of sugary sweets.

I will put in my box . . .
The *sound* of the wolves howling me to sleep,
And the *sound* of people diving into the swimming pool,
Zzzzzzz.

Andrew Jones (12)
Thomas Keble School

My Animal Alphabet

A The angry, agile ant,
who eats leaves and carries sticks all day.

B The big, booming beaver,
who lives in a wood and also eats wood.

C The crazy, caring cat,
who lives in a house and has five kittens to take care of.

D The dopey, drawling dog,
who lives in a basket and chases cats.

E The evil, elegant elephant,
who lives in a zoo and eats dung.

F The foul, foxy fox,
who lives in a forest and sleeps during the day.

G The gorgeous, galloping giraffe,
whose head hangs high above the trees.

H The humorous, hungry horse,
who was dying for something to eat.

I The icky, ill iguana,
who was home in bed being sick.

J The jumpy, jealous jaguar,
who was in a grump all day over a girl.

K The kind, kicking kangaroo,
who always was kicking herself with laughter.

L The laughing, leaping lion,
who was roaring at every stranger that went by.

M The mild, marvellous monkey,
who was the brainiest monkey I know.

N The nocturnal, neglecting newt,
who everyone ignored and neglected.

O The oblivious octopus,
who eats 8 things at a time and also does 8 things at a time.

P The polite, posh panda,
who always grooms herself before she goes out.

Q The quiet quail,
who never speaks or eats.

R The riot, raging rhino,
who as far as I know has never been in a good mood.

S The shy, silent seal,
who doesn't like to be around crowds.

T The tired, trailing tortoise,
   who always sleeps and it takes him five minutes to take 1 step.
U The unique unicorn,
   who nobody sees and always hopes to.
V The violent vole,
   who nobody goes near and is scared of.
W The worried whale,
   who was scared of everything and everyone.
X The xenophobia, xbee,
   who has a strong fear of everyone from different countries.
Y The yawning yak,
   who never actually wakes up and has been asleep for years.
Z The zany, zeal zebra,
   who is very humorous, and is very enthusiastic.

Ashton Harrison (11)
Thomas Keble School

How To Make Nathan Smith

Ingredients:
5 grumpy mornings.
A pile of blood.
8 kilograms of determination.
2 quick legs.
A dollop of excitement.
5 burgers.
4 doughnuts.
2 lay ins.
A football shirt.
1 chewed pen.

Method:
Firstly place 5 burgers into the mouth and stir well for about 2 minutes
Then add 8 kilograms of determination.
Add a dollop of excitement
And then put 2 quick legs on to the bottom of the body.
Then add a football shirt with four doughnuts
And stir for around 3 minutes.

Nathan Smith (11)
Thomas Keble School

How To Make Abi Wilkins

Ingredients:
1 loud laugh
A lot of clothes
4 episodes of 'Blossom'
1 bed
Plenty of lying in
7kg of confidence
5 tbs of sunshine
1 hairbrush
1 handful of shampoo
1 handful of conditioner
2kg milk chocolate.

Method:
Firstly take the loud laugh and mix in a lot of clothes.
Add the 4 episodes of 'Blossom'.
Slowly one at a time in a separate bowl mix 1 bed,
Lying in and add to the bowl.
Weigh 7kg of confidence and add along with 5tbs of sunshine.
Slowly place 1 hairbrush,
I handful of shampoo and 1 handful of conditioner.
Grate chocolate over top and mix all together.
Place in oven on baking tray
And cook on 180 degrees until light and fluffy.

Serving suggestion: pure friends.

Abi Wilkins (11)
Thomas Keble School

Lion

If I was a lion,
I would puff out my big, hairy chest
And roar and shout,
'I am the biggest and the best!'
Because I am the king,
With a big golden mane
Which shakes when I roar.

Alex Lata (11)
Thomas Keble School

What Makes Me 'Me'

There are lots of things that make me 'me'.

My parent's background,
And my genes.
My childhood,
And my family.

There are lots of things that make me 'me'.

My education,
The language I speak.
My accent,
And where I live.

There are lots of things that make me 'me'.

My friends at school,
The people I meet.
My personality,
And what I think.

There are lots of things that make me 'me'.

My dreams,
My feelings.
Thoughts are important too,
My future plans, what I will be.

There are lots of things that make me 'me',
These things are my identity.

Kelsey Ross (12)
Thomas Keble School

Horses

Horses are the best,
We're galloping very fast,
Then softly slow down.

The wind gets stronger,
We start to canter slowly,
Then suddenly *stop*.

Charlotte Maxwell (12)
Thomas Keble School

The White Tiger

I am a tiger and I can run as fast as a rocket.
I eat meat and all kinds of stuff.
I make a big roar, a loud growl.
I am a tiger who likes to sleep.
I am a tiger with a big black nose and massive claws.

I am a tiger who likes to run free.
I have two ears that hear your every move.
I am a tiger who likes to lie down.
I walk up and down by trees and rivers,
I like to have a wash and get mucky.

I also like to swim, I'm a bit like a crocodile sliding in the water,
I eat a bit of grass now and then to keep my strength up.
I am stripy and orange.
I have a long black tail, it goes to each side.

I am like a crocodile,
You can call me that if you like.

Samantha Green (11)
Thomas Keble School

About The School

The pupils of this school wear uniform,
The blue and black may seem boring.
Our individuality is calling!
We are made to tuck in T-shirts to conform.

Some of our lessons are very, very boring.
Some days on our timetable are extremely livid.
When teachers gets angry, they are vivid.
In geography I feel like snoring.

One day my T-shirt got pooped on by a seagull,
All my friends began to laugh and laugh,
As my friends did, so did the staff.
When I got home, I soaked it in the bath.

Danielle Dangerfield (13)
Thomas Keble School

Football

Football is the best sport ever to play.
Christiano Ronaldo is the best.
Most footballers that are freezing wear vests.
I love to play football on sunny days.

Arsenal are my least favourite team,
Leeds are in Division One.
Footy makes me glow like the shining sun,
Football matches give me joy of extreme.

Minchinhampton Rangers are the best ever.
Rugby is a game I don't enjoy at all.
When it comes to footy, I'm on the ball.
I have a big football madness fever.

I love and always will love watching my sport.
I love it when I am on the footy court.

Adam Loveridge (13)
Thomas Keble School

Nature Haikus

Tree
A cool rush of wind
Blows through the slender branches,
The lush green leaves sway.

Water
Trickling of water,
Drifting by the muddy bank,
Glistening in the sun.

Deer
Trotting through the trees,
A calm spring over the wall,
Trotting far away.

Gracie Fickling (11)
Thomas Keble School

Footy Poem

Footy is my favourite sport,
It is nothing like being on a tennis court.
A little bit of skill I'll go a long way,
I do that skill even though I have to pay.

When I score a goal,
I know that I am on the role.
I get all the sideline cheering me on,
That makes me eager to score more and more.

At the end of the match,
All covered in mud,
I am feeling great for making my team proud,
We have won the match
Which impresses the crowd.

Michael Ryan (13)
Thomas Keble School

Fisheye

If I was a fish, I would swim in tropical waters.
I would be a Siamese fighting fish defending my home.
I would protect my female from all others
And keep her my own.
When another male or predator came,
I would swish my fins and show my teeth
And bite to keep my honour.
I would find a rock with a large hole and lots of plants
And I would build a fabulous nest to live in.
If a human tried to catch me, I would dart and dodge
His clumsy hands and giggle with glee.
I am the king of the waters, I am my own boss.
I hunt by myself and eat other fish.

Ben Free (11)
Thomas Keble School

Turtle

I am
One of the slowest
Of all creatures.
Yep, the turtle.
That's me.
My droopy face
Completely lit up
By the sunlight,
A sight you would have to see.
Crowds of people surround my fantastic king,
Although we're not the only ones, mind.
Humungous leaves to chew at lunch,
Mmmm, munch, munch, munch.
My hard shell
Is as round as a football.
I'm a load better
Than any other animal!
Yep, the turtle,
That's me!

Brigida Anderson (12)
Thomas Keble School

Autumn

Autumn is my favourite season,
When all the leaves come off the trees.
Colours of burnt oranges and tree trunk browns,
The grounds all around us are like a mosaic,
Made by millions of colourful leaves.

It is the best time of the seasons to go for a walk,
In the woods and across some fields.
Autumn is my favourite season
And always it will be!

Jessica Cuddington (11)
Thomas Keble School

My Cat

I wake up in the morning, ready to feed my cat,
Then I hear a sound,
She's sat down on the mat.
She rushes down her food,
She knows I'm going to the park,
But she knows I won't be back until it gets dark.
So she waits and waits and hesitates.
I finally get back and go straight to bed.
She follows up the stairs,
Lies down with me and then I kiss her on the head.
She curls up nice and snuggly and warm,
And then we both wake up at dawn!

Billie Wiseman (11)
Thomas Keble School

Mouse

I am a mouse,
I hunt for cheese in the kitchens at night,
Trying not to be seen by cats and people.
I have a long, thin tail,
I am brown, not white.
My worst enemies are mouse traps and people.
I run along inside walls and on floors.
I live in a hole staying nice and warm.

Dale Cox (14)
Thomas Keble School

Limerick

There was an old man called Jake,
Who had a poisonous snake.
It bit his head
And now he's dead,
And that was the end of Jake.

Jamie Scott (12)
Thomas Keble School

My Goldfish

They swim around on their own
And they try to eat their only stone.

Guess what? I got hem a brand new toy
And they only went and called it Troy.

I watch them go around and around,
Swimming quietly without a sound.

Their names are Zack and Bettie,
Only because they look so pretty.

They are called bubble-eyed goldfish,
Because they give you just one wish.

I love my goldfish loads and load,
They make much better pets than smelly old toads.

Alex Bishop (13)
Thomas Keble School

A Horse

I stood alone in my stable
Wondering when I would be fed
The next bucket had my name on the label
Which lead to a grooming from Ted
Next out came the bridle and saddle
I'll be in trouble if I go for a paddle.

The smell of the grain over yonder
Is a sign that spring has begun
I can't help to stand and wonder
To be let loose in the field now would be fun
To feel the warm sun on my back
And to be free from all my tack.

Sabrina Cotterell (12)
Thomas Keble School

Who Am I?

Who am I?
I am a 12-year-old girl,
People say that I'm a chocoholic,
And I am a tall person.

Who am I?
I was born in Stroud,
My reports were good at school,
But I was a naughty toddler.

Who am I?
I have brown hair,
My bedroom is purple,
And my fish are called Fluffy and Spike!

Who am I?
I love animals,
Mum says my music is too loud,
My family all agree.

Who am I?
I really like shopping,
I like roast potatoes,
But cheese on toast is the best.

Who am I?
I go to judo club,
When I'm asked to I do the hoovering,
Sometimes I do my homework with the cat on my lap.

Who am I?
I live with my family,
Our home is in Chalford,
We're going on holiday soon.

Who am I?
I am happy,
I am cheerful,
I am very laid back (so they say.)

I am me!

Lizzy Warner (12)
Thomas Keble School

Not My Problem

(A poem in the style of Niyi Osundare)

She screamed at Ashley one day
Battered him soft like jelly
And shoved him down the throat
Of a waiting headmaster.
    What problem of mine is this
    As long as she doesn't take the pen
    From the grip of my working hand?

She came one evening
Thundered the whole house apart
And threw Daniel out
Then off to a lengthy isolation.
    What problem of mine is this
    As long as she doesn't take the pen
    From the grip of my working hand?

Dionne went to school open day
Only to find her class was gone
Without warning or query -
Just got bored and went away.
    What problem of mine is this
    As long as she doesn't take the pen
    From my working hand?

And then one evening
As I sat down to work
A knock on the door chilled my busy hand
She was waiting on my bemused front step
Shouting, shouting in her usual impatience.

Luke Pinkney (14)
Thomas Keble School

Not My Business

(A poem in the style of Niyi Osundare)

They took Mike away one night,
Bludgeoned him to a pulp,
And took him down the nick
Cause of shoplifting.
What responsibility of mine is it?
So long as I don't put a toe out of line
They won't come after me.

The classroom was the place,
Made the whole class gasp,
Swearing was the offence,
Poor David was out!
What responsibility of mine is it?
So long as I don't put a toe out of line
They won't come after me.

Paul was out one night
With some mates,
Picked on an Asian kid,
Got beaten up himself.
What responsibility of mine is it?
So long as I don't put a toe out of line
They won't come after me.

And then one day
As I was shopping,
The tannoy announced my name,
And the crime they said I made,
I pleaded I was innocent,
But everyone thought what business is it of mine.

Dan Browning (14)
Thomas Keble School

Why Should I Worry About It?

She bellowed loudly at Tara
And scared her stiff like wood,
And sent her away from prying eyes
To the corridor.
    Why should I worry about it?
    I just need to be good and quiet
    I've done nothing wrong.

He stormed in one lesson,
Everyone froze still,
And dragged poor Jimmy out
To a big and scary place.
    Why should I worry about it?
    I just need to be good and quiet
    I've done nothing wrong.

Hannah was loud one morning,
Having a laugh with her friends,
No warning, just a menacing voice,
A detention for a blame free girl.
    Why should I worry about it?
    I just need to be good and quiet
    I've done nothing wrong.

A letter came one morning,
My heart thumping like a drum,
I knew something was wrong,
Waiting, what could this be?

Clair Gittings (14)
Thomas Keble School

Turning A Blind Eye

They came at lunch
And picked up Mooney.
They shook him by the ankles
And took his lunch money.
It's alright as long as
I've got money and don't go hungry.

At break they came to Liam
And beat him black and blue
For his chocolate and Coke.
It's alright as long as
I've got money and don't go hungry.

Then the end, they went to Pete.
They beat him up bad
Just for his trainers.
They only got one.
It's alright as long as
I've got money and don't go hungry.

Oh no, here they come,
They came to me.
First the push to the wall,
Then the dreaded first hit.
They beat me senseless, I was out cold.

I wish I'd said something the first time.
Turning a blind eye.

Kester Birch (14)
Thomas Keble School

It's Her Problem

(A poem in the style of Niyi Osundare)

First day at school
And they picked her up and pulled her hair,
They kicked and punched and punched and kicked,
Until she bled like a piece of meat,
        It's not my business
        It's her problem
        Not mine!

They came the next break
And dragged her down to the waiting floor,
They screamed abuse
And kicked at her bleeding nose
        It's not my business
        It's her problem
        Not mine!

They came after school, this time
Nothing changed though
They stuffed mud in her face
Until she screamed for them to stop
        It's not my business
        It's her problem
        Not mine!

Then they stopped, had enough of her
They ran after me, they ran and ran
They caught me, and they kicked and punched
And punched and kicked
        It is my business
        It's not her problem
        It's mine!

Erika Lines (14)
Thomas Keble School

Not My Fault!

(A poem in the style of Niyi Osundare)

They swiftly closed down Ry,
He was drinking under age.
Threw him into the jaws
Of a waiting police car.
>   It's not my fault
>   I only had a bit
>   So they can't get me, can they?

They arrived one evening,
Caught Steve smoking a spliff.
They ushered him towards the door;
We didn't see him for a while.
>   It's not my fault
>   I only had a bit
>   So they can't get me, can they?

Will was vandalising things,
But people had seen it.
No questions were asked
Just reported to the police.
>   It's not my fault
>   I only did a bit
>   So they can't get me, can they?

And then one morning
I was still fast asleep,
A ring of the doorbell kicked my dormant brain.
The jaws were back
Still doing nothing, just waiting!

Tom Prosser (14)
Thomas Keble School

War

They picked Luke up one morning
Pounded him soft as dough
Then chucked him
In the jaws of the armoured truck.

Why should I bother?
So long as I wasn't
That unfortunate one!

They came one evening
Woke the house up with a *bang!*
And beat Paul down
Then they dragged him out.

Why should I bother?
So long as I wasn't
That unfortunate one!

Jamie went to college one day
Just to find that he was the one.
No alert, no warning, no letters
Only he was that one.

Why should I bother?
So long as I wasn't
That unfortunate one!

Then one night,
They came for me.
The knock on that door froze my sleeping head
There that van was again,
It was coming for me.

James Westerby (14)
Thomas Keble School

Why Should I Try And Help?

(A poem in the style of Niyi Osundare)

They cornered Robby after school
Took his money, ripped his shirt
And threw him on the unforgiving concrete
Of the pavement.
>Why should I try and help
>At least they won't take my money
>From my weak wallet?

They ambushed Harry one evening,
Took him down with baseball bats
And threatened him with flick knives
Wrenching his wallet from his shaking hand.
>Why should I try and help
>At least they won't take my money
>From my weak wallet?

Tom came back to his dorm one day
To find all his valuables gone
His clothes spread around
And his precious photos smashed.
>Why should I try and help
>At least they won't take my money
>From my weak wallet?

And then when I came out of class,
On my way to the shops
A hard tap on my shoulder petrified my body
The baneful concrete was inevitably waiting under my feet
Waiting, waiting in its usual stillness.

Joel Hunziker (14)
Thomas Keble School

How To Make Lucy Paton

Ingredients:
5 sprinkles of happiness.
A few dollops of art.
A few cups of hot water.
2 blue eyes.
A big portion of blonde hair.
A large 6kg of TV.
A handful of sweets
And one nutty girl.
A stupid giggle.
A silly laugh.
A big smile.
A drop of blue colouring.

Method:
Take the nutty girl and add the stupid giggle
And carefully place in a bowl, stir well.
Secondly, add the 2 blue eyes and the big potion of blonde hair.
Fold all ingredients careful, then add the few cups of hot water.
After it looks stupid add the silly laugh and the big smile.
Mix and fold into the mixture and then add 5 sprinkles of happiness.
Pour in the blue and yellow paint and the dollops of art.
Thirdly add the TV and cut up all the sweets
And pour them into the mixture, (without wrappers).
Cook the mixture until a laugh comes from the oven then it means it is ready.

Lastly, when it has come out, pour down the mouth
The blue colouring to make it sweeter.

Lucy Paton (11)
Thomas Keble School

An Animal Alphabet Poem

The angry, anxious alligator who pretended to be a log in the bog.
The buzzing busy bee who visited a flower and gave it to the queen.
The cowardly, crunching crocodile who swam all day.
The daring, devious dingo, who carries sharp teeth and claws.
The enormous, exciting elephant, who's grey and trumpets along.
The fearless, funky falcon, who flies and dives in the sky.
The great gallumping griffon who roars and rages despite his age.
The huffing, huge hippo who floated in the lake today.
The intelligent, interesting iguana who ate all the insects.
The jabbering, jumpy jaguar who climbed trees and didn't pay fees.
The kinky killer whale was 5,000 times bigger than a snail.
The lanky, lying lemur, lied and said a lot.
The mad, mooching monkey who rampaged through the town.
The naughty, nicking nautilus who lurked in the deep, deep sea.
The oblivious, obtuse octopus, who smirked at the fish.
The proud, powerful phoenix who bushed the bear.
The quirky queen quail gave orders and bossed everyone about.
The ruthless, reckless rat who was so secret he was quiet
                                                    as a mouse.
The scary, sociable seal who lived in the sea and played with me.
The teasing, toasting tiger who loved to play chase with the antelope.
The untrusting, unfaithful unicorn who had a horn when he was born.
The vicious, variable vole who drank too much ale and liked a snail.
The warm, wonderful warthog liked running round in circles.
The xylable xic who did nothing just like a stone
The young, youthful yabbie who lived in Australia, on the reef.
The zinging, zogging zebra who zapped Zulus in Africa.

Sam Driscoll (11)
Thomas Keble School